Practical **Strategies** for *Successful* Classrooms

Integrating Technology Into the Curriculum

Shelly Frei, Amy Gammill, M.Ed.,
and Sally Irons, M.Ed.

SHELL EDUCATION

Integrating Technology Into the Curriculum

Editor
Maria Elvira Kessler, M.A.

Project Manager
Maria Elvira Kessler, M.A.

Contributing Consultant
Marcia Russell, M.A.Ed.

Editor-in-Chief
Sharon Coan, M.S.Ed.

Creative Director
Lee Aucoin

Cover Design
Lee Aucoin
Lesley Palmer

Imaging
Phil Garcia
Don Tran

Publisher
Corinne Burton, M.A.Ed.

Shell Education
5301 Oceanus Drive
Huntington Beach, CA 92649-1030
www.shelleducation.com
ISBN 978-1-4258-0379-7
©*2007 Shell Education*
Made in U.S.A.

Table of Contents

Table of Contents *(cont.)*

Table of Contents *(cont.)*

Table of Contents *(cont.)*

Introduction

Jump back in time to 1992. What was your personal technology experience as a student or a teacher? Were there computers in your school? Maybe your school had a few Apple II computers in a small lab or in the library. Students probably had limited access to them and most likely no access to the Internet or high-quality software programs.

Now jump forward to 2006. Most schools have fast graphic-laden computers with Internet access. Maybe you have a few computers in your classroom. Certainly you have a television or access to one. You may also have access to a computer projector and other tools of technology. What you may not have access to, however, are the knowledge and experience to use these wonderful tools of technology to further student learning.

Across the United States and around the globe for the past decade, teachers at all grade levels have faced a common dilemma: how to teach and apply technology effectively in the classroom. The solution is not as simple as placing a computer in a classroom and allowing students to use it. In fact, there is a more exciting prospect: teachers can harness the computer and other forms of technology as tools for learning. Moreover, this learning can develop the higher-order thinking and problem-solving skills that students will need to succeed in our fast-paced, information-saturated world.

As a teacher, the dilemma is threefold. Not only are teachers expected to teach students how to use technology, but teachers must also find ways for students to use technology to learn. Furthermore, teachers are faced with the task of utilizing technology for their own organizational and administrative purposes. Not surprisingly, the technological learning curve for most teachers is steep. Teachers, experienced and new, often feel overwhelmed by the challenges that technology brings to their classrooms. To compound the problem, teachers must often learn how to integrate technology into their classrooms on their own time.

In this book, we hope you will find practical ideas and resources to help you integrate technology into your classroom. The ideas and exercises we share in this book are based on solid research and proven methodology. There is no need to reinvent the wheel. Many teachers and administrators have faced this challenge before you. We hope to draw upon their experiences to enable you to harness technology for yourself and your students.

Organization of the Book

As you proceed through the book, you will find it to be different from most. Most notably, it is interactive. Each chapter begins with a pre-reading review designed to check the reader's knowledge, which will give you some insight as to what the chapter will cover. At the end of each chapter, there are chapter reflections to help you integrate the addressed aspect of technology into your classroom. The organization and elements of the book make it highly valuable and accessible for collegial professional development activities. Teachers gain even further insight by discussing the material together and collaborating on the interactive activities.

Each chapter of this book addresses a different component of classroom technology integration. **Chapter One** provides the overall methodology and vision for how to best integrate technology into your classroom. It discusses the teacher as a coach and the computer as a tool for learning. **Chapter Two** focuses on the ISTE NETS for Teachers and the ISTE NETS for Students. These are the national technology standards for teachers and students that were developed by the International Society for Technology in Education. **Chapter Three** focuses on software programs. It presents a variety of different ways in which to incorporate word processing, spreadsheets, databases, desktop publishing, and multimedia into classroom lessons and activities. **Chapter Four** addresses the Internet and all it has to offer. It covers everything from effectively searching and evaluating Internet Web pages and creating Hotlists, WebQuests, and Internet Projects to communicating through email, chat rooms, and instant messaging. **Chapter Five** focuses on using technology for assessments and evaluation. **Chapter Six** concentrates on using technology to assist with classroom management and administration. It explores online and electronic grade book programs, computer scheduling, classroom layout, and technological gadgets, with an emphasis on rubrics, online testing, and ePortfolios. **Chapter Seven** covers the basics of computer troubleshooting. This chapter outlines the minor problems that teachers run into when dealing with input and output devices, printers, viruses, spyware, and malware. **Chapter Eight** addresses technology and professional development. It showcases the vast number of online courses and tutorials that are available to educators, as well as a number of technology-based publications. **Chapter Nine** covers the topic of technology funding. It addresses what a grant is and how to write an effective proposal. Finally, appendices at the end of the book neatly organize some useful online student and teacher resources for quick reference.

Teacher as Coach, Computer as the Tool

Pioneers in the use of computers and other technology in education have much to teach us about integrating technology into our classrooms. It is through their expertise, experience, observation, research, and discussion that we can learn how to best make use of the power of today's technology to teach our students.

Technology in the classroom is nothing new to education. In the past, computers were used mainly as a tool to teach basic skills through the use of "drill and kill" software. There is a place for those programs that focus on basic skills, but educators are realizing the potential that computers have to help improve their students' education.

Check Your Knowledge

Directions: Evaluate the accuracy of each statement below. Place a T (for True) or an F (for False) in the spaces provided.

_____ 1. The use of technology in the classroom encourages the traditional role of teacher as lecturer.

_____ 2. The use of technology in the classroom supports teachers in encouraging students to use higher-order thinking skills.

_____ 3. Technology can be used to enhance learning when teachers put the technology into students' hands and challenge them to apply it to solve problems and complete projects.

_____ 4. Even when the teacher acts as coach, sometimes the teacher needs to share important pre-knowledge before a project is presented to students.

_____ 5. The term *information literate* is used to describe a student or teacher who looks to the media for solutions to problems.

_____ 6. Technology and popular culture have slowed down the delivery of information and decreased the quantity of information available to students.

_____ 7. A teacher who seeks to incorporate technology into his/her classroom to develop information literate students must provide interesting and relevant projects, questions, and problems for students to undertake.

_____ 8. Computers are not teachers in and of themselves.

_____ 9. Computers should be integrated into the curriculum as much as possible.

_____ 10. The teacher as coach role also includes differentiating the lesson for students of varied abilities.

Teacher as Coach

The modern-day classroom is now moving beyond utilizing computers to simply teach students basic skills. In a research report on media and technology, Thomas Reeves made a distinction on the use of technology by clarifying the difference between "learning from" and "learning with" technology. Learning from technology implies the computer is acting as a tutor delivering instruction on basic skills. Traditionally, this has been the way technology was used in the classroom. Learning with computers implies that the computer is a tool to solve problems where students must gather, organize, and analyze problems. This approach supports constructivist teachings and the idea that technologies are cognitive tools that can be used to expand on student learning (Reeves, 1998). With the expectation that students be information literate, educators need to spend more time designing lessons where students are learning with computers rather than from them. Using the computer as a tool provides students with the opportunity to develop and use their higher-level thinking skills to solve problems that are relevant to their daily lives. As we move toward the idea of learning with technology, teachers are taking on a new role in the classroom. Hobbs (2006) points out in addition to simply bringing students access to online sources, such as online newspapers, magazine articles, and blogs, K–12 educators are now "involving students in creating their own messages using visual, electronic and digital media tools" (p. 16).

Technology lends itself to a new role for the teacher: that of facilitator and coach. Replacing the traditional model of a teacher as a lecturer, the teacher instead presents students with challenging real-life problems and the technology tools to solve them (Means & Olson, 1994). It is significant that as teachers take on the role of coach, students also take on a new role: that of active participants. In a research study that focused on project-based learning with multimedia, participant teachers reported the shift in their roles in the classroom. They found they were less likely to lecture and more likely to facilitate or coach students (Penuel, Golan, Means, & Korbak, 2000). A teacher acting as a coach can now join his/her students in the learning process, encouraging them to use technology tools to help overcome any obstacles they may face when trying to find a solution. In the end, the teacher helps students draw conclusions and assess their learning. In these activities, the teacher encourages students to use higher-order thinking skills with scaffolding provided through the highly motivational technology tools. "Teaching higher-order thinking skills involves not so much conveying information as conveying understanding. Students learn concepts and then attempt to apply them to various problems, or they solve problems and then learn the concepts that underlie the solutions" (Wenglinsky, 2002, Background section, para. 7). The use of technology supports teachers in this lofty goal.

The teacher as coach model is not new. Most likely you have assumed this role when you have challenged students to solve problems or complete interesting projects. You likely already know that cognitive research shows that learning improves when students are actively involved in learning, working in groups, frequently interacting and receiving feedback, and seeing the connections to real life (Roschelle, Pea, Hoadley, Gordin, & Means, 2001). What might be new to you is what experts like Jamie McKenzie have discovered over the past decade—*the teacher as coach, computer as a tool* model is the best methodology for effective integration of technology into the classroom (McKenzie, 2000). In other words, technology is best used to enhance learning when teachers put the technology into students' hands and challenge them to apply it to solve problems and complete projects.

Table 1.1 summarizes the differences between the traditional role of a teacher and the teacher as coach model.

Table 1.1: Teacher as Coach vs. Traditional Teacher

Teacher as Coach	Traditional Teacher
• Designs projects and/or problems for students to tackle • Asks thought-provoking, open-ended questions to guide students • Provides tools and teaches students how to use them to solve problems • Modifies lessons for higher-ability and lower-ability students • Forms cooperative groups; willing to change direction of lesson based on student interest • Evaluates skills, effort, and knowledge using a combination of assessment devices • Leads students through self-assessment processes	• Presents information lecture-style • Demonstrates skills and directs students to mimic the steps • Shows students how to solve problems • Leads students to one "right" answer • Favors having students work on their own • Evaluates students almost exclusively with paper-and-pencil tests

A Word About Lectures

Occasionally, teachers still need to share information with students in the traditional lecture-style. Oftentimes, the teacher needs to share important pre-knowledge before a project is presented to students. The main idea of the teacher as coach model is to ensure that a great deal of the instruction is student-centered, with students being active problem solvers and learners. This is why technology is so exciting. Technology lends itself to project- or problem-based lessons.

Helping to Create Information Literate Students

Part of the teacher as coach model is helping to create information literate students. The term *information literate* is used to describe a student or teacher who knows how to question, think independently, invent, research, and problem solve. "As America moves toward an information society, critical thinking skills, problem-solving skills, and competence in information literacy in order to process information become increasingly more important for all students" ("Information Literacy in an Information Society," 1994, p. 4). Technology and popular culture have accelerated the delivery of information and increased the quantity of information available to students. Information literate students do not simply regurgitate information. They do not immediately believe what they read. They skim, discriminate, question, analyze, and synthesize information. This is why it is so important that we create learning situations in which students are not merely instructed, lectured, or shown how to do something.

Internet researcher Dan Tapscott notes that while much of the world is controlled by adults, with kids as passive spectators, the Internet gives students an opportunity to not just observe, but also to participate (Tapscott, 1998). We must prepare students for an information-saturated world, a world where adaptable thinking and solid problem-solving skills are paramount for success and, in some cases, survival. As a teacher, you have the unique opportunity to provide your students with opportunities to practice questioning and problem solving, as well as using technology tools to solve problems, answer questions, and communicate. In this way, you will help to create students who are information literate and, eventually, citizens who can navigate and succeed in our increasingly complex world.

Questions, Problems, Projects—
Meaningful Uses of Technology

In the past, the teacher and texts were the only sources of knowledge for any given content area. Technology brings more exciting, up-to-date, and diverse materials right into the classroom (Hawkins, 1997). A teacher who seeks to integrate technology into his/her classroom to develop information literate students must provide interesting, relevant projects, questions, and problems for students to tackle. So what are project-based or problem-based lessons that engage students in real-life tasks and build critical thinking skills? Such lessons begin with a question or problem that is meaningful to students because it will send them on an interesting, challenging investigation. Examples of questions and problems include:

- What pattern do you see in the multiples of six? (3rd grade)

- How are the oral traditions of the Ashanti from Africa and the Pawnee Native Americans similar and different? (5th grade)

- Why did kings and queens live in castles? (Kindergarten)

- Does tap water have the same pH level and contain the same metals in different cities in the United States? (6th–8th grade)

- What is your opinion regarding the U.S. Supreme Court's ruling in favor of George W. Bush in the 2000 Presidential Election? (8th grade)

- How many students in our classroom like chocolate chip ice cream? Rocky Road? Mint chip? (1st grade)

It is important to note that all of the above questions were formed to address academic standards and can be answered (or conclusions can be presented) with the help of technology. So, how can students use technology to help answer questions like those above? Here are some examples of projects involving technology:

- Brainstorm the answer to a question using graphical organizing software.

- Create a collective class database to collect information on a history, science, math, or language arts topic.

- Discover patterns in multiples of numbers using a calculator.

- Research literature, ancient and modern cultures, scientific discoveries, historical events, mathematical history, famous artworks, geological data, etc., using the Internet.

- Participate in real scientific research using the Internet.

- Communicate (using email) with other classrooms across the United States and the world to collect scientific or sociological data.

- Create newsletters, invitations, and posters using word processing software to synthesize and apply knowledge and ideas.

- Construct a persuasive multimedia presentation as the culmination of a research project.

- Use a spreadsheet program to organize economic data and create graphs to compare that data.

In the next section, you will see an example of a new teacher directing her students in a project-based lesson that incorporates technology as a tool used to complete the project.

Teacher as Coach in a Lesson Integrating Technology

The Scenario

Sophie, a new teacher, wishes to address some of the technology and science standards her district expects her to teach her fifth-grade students. She has two computers in her classroom and access to 20 more computers in a computer lab. Each computer in her classroom and in the lab has word processing, spreadsheet, multimedia, desktop publishing, and drawing software programs, as well as Internet access.

The Project

Realizing that being a new teacher is a challenge by itself, Sophie wisely decides to borrow a lesson idea from another teacher. In this case, she goes online and finds a standards-based lesson on an education website. The lesson poses the following question to students: How is the geology of Earth similar to or different from the geology of the moon? Students assume the roles of either geologists or astrogeologists to investigate the physical characteristics of Earth and the moon. Students are to work in pairs and use their own observations, the Internet, and books to collect their information. They are given a chart which directs them to record what they find and sources of information they consulted. Once they have collected their information, students meet with a group that conducted the opposite research (i.e., the geologists meet with the astrogeologists). At these meetings they discuss what is similar and different about the geology of Earth and the moon and record the information from the other group on the backs of their papers. Then, they are instructed to create a table in a word processing document and then a Venn Diagram on paper comparing the physical characteristics of Earth and the moon.

Days One Through Five of the Project

Before beginning, Sophie decides to tweak the lesson a little to fit the unique needs of her students. She decides, for example, that her students need to know a little more about conducting research on the Internet before the lesson. She spends **day one** in the computer lab showing students how to use a kid-friendly search engine to find information. She uses a computer projector attached to the teacher's computer to show students the steps. Then Sophie gives them time to practice on their own.

In the computer lab on **day two**, Sophie asks the students to recall from previous lessons the definitions of the terms *geology* and *physical characteristics*. She then uses the computer projector to show the students pictures of Earth and the moon. Next, Sophie asks the students to spend time in small groups discussing and writing down their hypotheses for the question: How is the geology of Earth similar to or different from the geology of the moon? Then she assigns the pairs of students to either the role of geologist or astrogeologist. She pairs students who are more familiar with technology with those who are less experienced. She asks what the differences are between geologists and astrogeologists; students discuss this in small groups before offering suggestions. She tells students to use the Internet to find the physical characteristics of either Earth or the moon, depending on their assignment. While they are looking for information, Sophie walks around the classroom, listens to the students talking and working, and peeks at their computer screens. She assists students by talking them through any obstacles. She provides information when necessary to scaffold the lesson for struggling students. However, she resists the temptation to lead them directly to the answers.

On **day three** back in the classroom, Sophie provides geology books of varied complexity to students and presses them to find more physical characteristics of Earth or the moon. For those students with a complete list, she challenges them to choose one physical characteristic, predict how it was formed, and then find the answer using a classroom computer or a book. After students are given a little time, Sophie then directs pairs of students to meet and share their research. She explains that this is what scientists do: they share their research in order to further everyone's knowledge and build upon existing knowledge. The pairs then exchange their research.

On **day four** back in the computer lab, Sophie uses the computer projector to briefly remind her students how to create a table in a word processing document, which is a skill her students had learned in a previous lesson. The students are creating tables to display their research and the research of the other group.

On **day five**, students work by themselves to create Venn Diagrams on paper, comparing and contrasting the physical characteristics of Earth and the moon. Sophie assists students who need help to complete their diagrams. As the students finish, they meet with other students who are finished to discuss their findings. Finally, students explain in writing how their original hypotheses were correct or incorrect. They are also told to think of reasons why the physical characteristics of Earth and the moon are similar or different. Students with time to spare are encouraged to use the classroom computers and books to explore this final question further. When everyone is finished, the class comes together to discuss that final question.

Computer as the Tool

In the lesson above, you can see that Sophie did not rely on the computers to teach her students. She did not sit them down in front of the computers and have the students use a software program to learn facts or skills.

Computers are not teachers. When technology is used as a tool, the students and teachers are in control of their learning and the direction their learning takes. Using computers as a tool allows students to use higher-level thinking skills to solve problems (Means et al., 1993). The power of technology lies with how the teacher uses it. As in Sophie's classroom, the computer acted as a tool for students to explore and gather information to support a problem-based project. Think of a computer as you would a pencil, ruler, compass, or microscope. We do not expect these implements to teach skills or knowledge to students. We use them with students as tools to help students make new discoveries and solve problems.

Software that facilitates critical thinking and higher-order thinking works best with the teacher as coach, computer as tool model. Using these tools helps students to question, plan, gather, analyze, and report. Examples of these software programs include databases, word processors, spreadsheets, multimedia presentation programs, publishing programs, and graphic organizing programs (Reeves, 1998). See Chapter Three for more information on how to use these programs in your classroom.

Of course, there is an *occasional* place for allowing students to use computer programs that help reinforce learning already taking place in the classroom. Instructional software programs that help students practice math facts or new vocabulary can be helpful when used now and then. Some high quality programs, like *The Logical Journey of the Zoombinis*, can also lead students through problem-solving exercises that involve logic and reasoning.

When planning a lesson incorporating software, remember that teaching students how to use the program is not enough. Think about why the students are using the program. What project can they accomplish? What question or problem can they solve when they use the program to create a product? In the above lesson example, students first used the Internet to collect information and help answer a question. Then they used a word processing program to create a table to compare their research to another group's research.

Computers Integrated, Not Isolated

Related to the above idea that computers are tools and not teachers is the important idea that technology skills should not be taught in isolation. Computers should be integrated into the curriculum as much as possible. They are best used by students to solve real-life problems and to complete meaningful projects (Eisenberg & Johnson, 2002). A computer lab full of computers running instructional software programs, where students go regularly to do drill-and-kill exercises is *not* a good use of such powerful tools.

Research suggests that when technology is integrated throughout the curriculum, students will not only learn technology skills but also content knowledge (Silverstein, Frechtling, & Miyaoka, 2000). Integrating computers throughout the curriculum enables students to develop the skills needed to be successful in the workplace, including locating and accessing information, organizing data, and making persuasive arguments (Sandholtz, Ringstaff, & Dwyer, 1997). To set up a computer lab with a lab instructor who teaches computer skills in isolation from academic standards or meaningful projects is not an effective use of technology. "How can anyone justify spreadsheeting divorced from real questions as a worthwhile endeavor? Or PowerPointing? Or Internetting?" (McKenzie, 2000). In the same vein, do not be drawn in (or let your principal or lab coordinator be drawn in) by the temptation to purchase and follow a sequential, self-contained, isolated technology curriculum. Such programs waste money and academic time and do not encourage students to think critically. An analogy would be setting up a science tool lab, where students spend one hour per week learning how to use microscopes, Bunsen burners, pipettes, etc., without actually making connections to real scientific issues. Computers, just like microscopes, should be used for investigations, analysis, data collection, and problem solving in the context of a meaningful question, problem, or project.

If your school is lucky enough to have a dedicated computer lab instructor, then he/she should work closely with the teacher to deliver lessons in the computer lab that are intimately tied to what you are doing in the classroom. Work with your school's computer lab instructor to create lessons that teach computer skills as a means to completing a project or creating a product (Eisenberg & Johnson, 2002).

Ways to Differentiate with Technology in a Lesson

The teacher as coach role also includes differentiating the lesson for students of varied abilities. Most classes have a wide variety of skill ranges, whether related to content skill or technology skill. Recognizing that students have differing abilities in technology and problem solving, the teacher can modify the lesson appropriately for individual students. There are many ways to differentiate instruction to meet the varied ability levels of students. Here we focus on the methods that are relevant to projects that incorporate technology.

Use Student Grouping

In the scenario on the previous pages, Sophie grouped students in different ways during the lesson. Working in pairs or teams on challenging projects is an excellent way to promote learning and higher-order thinking. When using the tools of technology to research or solve problems together, students will discuss, brainstorm, build on each other's ideas, and find solutions. This collaboration is teaching them higher-order thinking skills and the value of working together and will prepare them for the world outside of school. Having computers in the classroom actually promotes collaboration. It has been found that students with access to computers actually work together more than in classrooms without computers (Apple, 1995). The teacher as coach role means that the teacher strategically plans the groups for any technology project. At times, students of similar ability are paired or included in the same group, but more often, students of mixed ability are grouped together. Another way to differentiate using student groupings is to have students work in pairs or teams for part of a project or assignment but then work individually for other parts of the assignment. For example, students can work together to research and collect data but work by themselves to organize or display the data. Similarly, some students can work in teams and others by themselves on a particular task, depending on their abilities to complete the task alone.

Monitor Reading Ability

In the teacher as coach role, the teacher needs to monitor the reading ability of various students who are engaged in technology research. For example, if students are using the Internet to research a subject, you wouldn't want your lowest readers struggling through a university-level Ph.D. dissertation that they found online. The teacher should gently guide students to find research that is at the appropriate reading and age level. Another way to differentiate is to provide resources of varied reading and complexity levels (Willis & Mann, 2000). Seek out books and websites of varying reading levels and complexity before beginning a project to provide the necessary resources to students.

Display of Information Found

Technology allows students to search for and display information in different ways. One group may decide to summarize their information by using a word-processing program. Another group may decide to create a chart using a spreadsheet. Another group may decide to make a slide show presentation of their information. The teacher as coach can encourage creativity in the display of information. This teacher as coach role also applies to making sure students understand the ethics involved in using copyrighted material in their display of researched information.

Extend the Lesson for Higher-Ability Levels

A great way to challenge higher-ability students is to extend a lesson with an open-ended question. In the example lesson above, Sophie extends the lesson for students who have completed their assignments by posing the question: Why are the physical characteristics of Earth and the moon similar or different? Students are encouraged to use books or a classroom computer to explore this question while the rest of the class finishes the original task.

The next chapter outlines the national technology education standards that provide the framework for student learning using technology.

Chapter One Reflection

1. Describe some of the differences between the teacher as coach and traditional teacher models of instruction.

   _____

   _____

   _____

2. Describe an information literate student. Why is it important that students become information literate?

   _____

   _____

   _____

3. Think of a lesson that you have taught, observed, or read about that incorporated technology. In what ways could this lesson be modified to differentiate for lower-ability students? How might you differentiate the lesson for higher-ability students?

   _____

   _____

   _____

4. Describe how incorporating technology into the classroom can help you provide project- and problem-based lessons to students.

   _____

   _____

   _____

Technology Standards for Teachers and Students

The previous chapter looked at the overall methodology for using technology to enhance students' learning experiences. This chapter takes a closer look at the technology objectives that guide your decisions when planning lessons.

The National Education Technology Standards (NETS)

Every lesson is based upon learning objectives. A teacher generates learning objectives in order to help students achieve mastery in the content standards required for a particular curriculum area by the district or the state.

Sometimes, the standards come from professional educational organizations such as the International Society for Technology in Education (ISTE). ISTE developed standards for technology education called the National Educational Technology Standards (NETS) that set the bar for schools across the nation. According to the ISTE website, as of May 19, 2004, 48 out of 50 states, and the District of Columbia, have adopted, adapted, or referenced the National Educational Technology Standards for Teachers, Students, and Administrators in their states' technology plans, within their curriculum development, and in other state documents.

The National Educational Technology Standards explain what teachers, administrators, and students should know and be able to do with regard to technology. Use the NETS for Teachers to guide your own professional development. The NETS for Teachers will tell you what you need to know to successfully integrate technology into your classroom. Use the NETS for Students in conjunction with your district or state technology standards to plan your lessons and assess your students.

Why Is There a Need for Technology Standards?

At a time when most states are requiring teachers to adapt to standard-driven education in all subject areas, there is a call for technology to be included as well. The CEO Forum on Education and Technology, a partnership of business and education leaders founded in 1996, spent five years analyzing how well the educational field integrated technology into its curriculum. Agreeing that there was a critical need for students to be on the forefront of the newest technology available, they offered the following recommendations to federal policymakers. The policy paper requested that the Department of Education include technology into standards-based curriculum, expand federal support for technology integration, and continue to research the development and dissemination of technological advances. "The Department of Education should establish accountability models for the inclusion of 21st century skills as an additional discipline" (CEO Forum, 2001, p. 5). By creating the accountability that standards provide, students receive the necessary skills to become global citizens for the future. Jan Hawkins, who served as director for a nonprofit research group called the Center for Children and Technology in New York, noted that there is a need for the schools to catch up with technology use in the business world (Hawkins, 1997). She made an appeal for accountability because of the types of technology-based jobs available at that time. The rise of the technology-based job market has only grown since then. The inclusion of technology standards in the curriculum is indispensable to preparing students of all ages for the real world, especially as technology develops even further.

This chapter takes a detailed look at the ISTE NETS for Teachers and the ISTE NETS for Students. You will also have the opportunity to evaluate your own skills and to compare them against the standards for teachers. You will be asked to review the student standards and estimate the proficiency level of a group of students that you either work with or have worked with in the past. Before you begin reading about the ISTE NETS for Teachers and Students, assess your knowledge of the technology skills in the ISTE NETS and your knowledge of the use of technology standards in education.

Check Your Knowledge

Directions: Evaluate the accuracy of each statement below. Place a T (for True) or an F (for False) in the space provided.

_____ 1. Teachers of all grade levels must design and teach technology-enhanced lessons that incorporate the student technology standards.

_____ 2. Technology standards are used as guidelines to ensure that teachers and students have important technology skills.

_____ 3. Teachers should remain current on their school district's Acceptable Use Policy and other ethical policies that focus on educational technology.

_____ 4. PreK–12th grade students need to understand the ethical uses of technology.

_____ 5. Teachers should incorporate technology as a separate time period in the school day.

_____ 6. All PreK–12th grade students should be able to generate a developmentally appropriate word processor document.

_____ 7. The student performance indicators, which come from the ISTE NETS for Students, should be the same for all grade levels.

_____ 8. Collaboration is not an important component of the ISTE NETS for Students performance indicators for PreK–12th grade students.

_____ 9. There are very few resources for teachers who are trying to develop lessons based on the ISTE NETS for Students.

_____ 10. Teachers should ignore their own district or state technology standards and instead use the ISTE NETS to develop lessons and assess students.

ISTE National Education Technology Standards (NETS) for Teachers

The International Society of Technology Educators (ISTE), with the help of a consortium of other stakeholders, developed the National Educational Technology Standards for Teachers (NETS for Teachers) in the early 1990s. The ISTE NETS for teachers was developed to ensure that educators have a solid foundation in technology in order to be effective teachers of technology. It is ISTE's continued belief that "[t]oday's classroom teachers must be prepared to provide technology-supported learning opportunities for their students. Being prepared to use technology and knowing how that technology can support student learning must become integral skills in every teacher's professional repertoire" (ISTE, 2002, p. 4). It is extremely important that teachers realize that there are technology standards to which they must hold themselves accountable.

Let's take a closer look at the NETS for teachers. The NETS for teachers are organized into six categories:

1. **Technology Operations and Concepts.** These standards address the teacher's understanding of basic technology issues and ability to learn about technology as it changes and develops.

2. **Planning and Designing Learning Environments and Experiences.** These standards address the teacher's ability to create effective learning environments that utilize technology.

3. **Teaching, Learning, and the Curriculum.** These standards address the teacher's ability to use appropriate strategies to maximize student learning experiences while using technology.

4. **Assessment and Evaluation.** These standards address the teacher's ability to use technology in the assessment of students.

5. **Productivity and Professional Practice.** These standards address the teacher's ability to use technology in professional activities, including further professional development and communication with colleagues, parents, and the community.

6. **Social, Ethical, Legal, and Human Issues.** These standards address the teacher's ability to adhere to the social, ethical, legal, and human issues surrounding technology use in schools.

Each of the six standards areas is broken down into performance indicators that more specifically explain proficiency in that area. A complete description of the different standards, performance indicators, and performance profiles can be found on the ISTE website (*http://www.iste.org*).

More Than Technology Skills

Notice that there is much more to the NETS for teachers than possessing key technology skills. To be proficient in the NETS for teachers, you must be able to plan and execute lessons involving meaningful uses of technology. You must also be able to assess student proficiency in technology and use technological tools to assess students. Furthermore, you must use technology to help manage your classroom and accomplish organizational tasks. Finally, you must be aware and apply your understanding of the social, ethical, legal, and human issues associated with technology used in an educational setting. It is also very important that you and your students follow the guidelines and rules outlined in your school district's Acceptable Use Policy (AUP). The AUP is a document that all computer users in a school or school district, including students, must sign. By signing the document, the computer user agrees to follow the rules and ethical practices that ensure proper use of the school's or school district's computers and networks. The standards make it clear that students of all ages should abide by the appropriate guidelines.

Dave and Marilyn Forest, teachers from Union City, California, recently became nationally board-certified teachers. They believe that "if we're ever going to improve the perception of teachers in the country, we'll have to start raising the standards" (Forrest & Forrest, 2001, para. 5). Both of them integrated technology into their professional activities and their curriculum in order to demonstrate that they were worthy of this highly prestigious certification. Their use of technology extended across each of the NETS mentioned above. They videotaped many of their own lessons and used various computer programs to organize data collection. In order to demonstrate the social science requirements to show that students make connections to the real world, one of Dave's projects involved having his history students interview someone who had lived through an important historical event. He then posted the interviews on the Internet. Marilyn developed a computer program to help her English class relate to the literature they were reading and respond in powerful ways, such as writing a response in poetry. Additionally, in an effort to help teachers teach technology embedded in content and not in isolation, Marilyn created curriculum programs with computer-based lesson ideas (Forrest & Forrest, 2001). Marilyn isn't alone. Many accomplished teachers are writing lessons for educational websites designated for teacher use. All it takes is a search engine, and any teacher can have a handful of innovative, creative, standards-based ideas at his/her fingertips.

For now, start by assessing your basic technology skills to gain a clearer picture of what you can do on a computer. Table 2.1 shows a basic list of essential computer skills that teachers should have.

Table 2.1: Essential Computer Skills for Teachers

- Know the basic hardware components of a computer
- Use the online help function within software applications
- Understand how different passwords are generated and used
- Know about basic file structure and manipulation (i.e., what a folder is and how to copy, move, and delete a file on a hard drive or disk)
- Know how to search for a file and how to select a location when saving from the Internet or an email attachment
- Know the basics of the computer's operating system
- Know how to send and receive email
- Know how to use the Internet
- Be able to integrate technology-based grade level/content lessons into classroom activities
- Run antivirus software
- Use a word processor and its basic functions
- Save and retrieve files
- Manage data in teacher-based productivity software (i.e., grade book, attendance, etc.)
- Know and use proper computer terminology
- Be able to follow written and oral instructions to complete computer tasks
- Use common sense and have realistic expectations when using a computer
- Be willing to try to figure out problems that arise when using technology
- Know how to check for unplugged or loose cables
- Realize that sometimes computers do unexpected things and a reboot often fixes the problem
- Report a computer/technology problem to the person or persons who have the capability to fix it

Improving Your Personal Technology Skills

At this point, you may be wondering how you can enhance your current technology skills and learn new skills in many of the areas listed in Table 2.1. Having computers in the classroom that are ready for use may be overwhelming for you. You may desire specific training in the application of using them within your lessons. Professional development is readily available for willing teachers.

Professional development ideally should include intensive exploratory training sessions, follow-up support over time, ongoing dialogue amongst colleagues, and observation of other teachers (Hawkins, 1997). Sometimes a group of teachers can ask the administration to bring experts to staff meetings for training. However, staff meetings frequently tend to deal with day-to-day issues rather than professional development. Teacher expertise is a significant determinant of student success, and teachers need focused staff development to build competence in new areas. Teachers should ask about available district technology workshops. In larger districts, technology experts may be available to answer questions and address concerns with a simple phone call.

A teacher may choose to take a course at the local community college as well. Technology courses are usually offered regularly throughout the year. In an effort to tackle the technology issue head on, a teacher may want to try an online course to learn more about technology while using it. Another way to use technology in the search for learning more about it is to videotape other teachers and learn from their integration of technology. There are many books written on improving technology skills; many are even written specifically for self-professed beginners. Teachers can also use search engines (e.g., Yahoo! and Google) to search the Internet for resources and further coaching. A teacher can type "teacher technology" and find many interesting sites to explore. These sites might give technology training, as well as specific lesson plans and ideas for technology use in the classroom. If a teacher searches the Internet for the specific content subject, such as life science, teaching-related sites will often have ways to integrate technology into the curriculum. Finally, the best resource for teachers is other teachers. Your colleagues are often enthusiastic about sharing technology ideas, advice, and experience. There is more guidance about this topic in Chapter Eight of this book.

Get a Clearer Picture for Lessons and Professional Development

You may be comfortable with only some of the skills listed in Table 2.1. Believe it or not, you will be able to incorporate technology into your lessons no matter what your skill level. See the section in this chapter titled "Developing Lessons Using Technology Standards" (page 47) for an explanation of how to integrate technology skills into your lessons a few at a time.

Use the survey on page 39 to more accurately assess your skill level. After completing the survey, you will have a better idea of those skills with which you feel comfortable enough to introduce to your students. This rubric will also give you an idea of skills on which you can focus for your own professional development.

Teacher Skills Survey

Directions: Please indicate your comfort level with each of the following technology skills.

Technology Skills:	Can't do this	Can do with assistance	Can do independently	Can teach others
Identify basic hardware components (e.g., monitor, keyboard, mouse, system unit, printer, scanner)				
Understand and use correct computer terminology				
Troubleshoot and repair simple hardware/software problems				
Manage files (e.g., copy, move, delete)				
Search for, save, and retrieve a file				
Save files in a user-specified location (e.g., downloading files from the Internet and email)				
Use the online help function within software applications				
Understand how different passwords are generated and used				
Remove computer viruses and spyware				
Use word processing software (e.g., Microsoft Word)				
Use spreadsheet software (e.g., Microsoft Excel)				
Use Database software (e.g., Microsoft Access)				
Use multimedia presentation software (e.g., Microsoft PowerPoint)				
Use desktop publishing software (e.g., Microsoft Publisher)				
Use instructional software (e.g., MathBlaster or CCC Math)				
Use email (e.g., send, retrieve, create, and open attachments)				
Use a Web browser (e.g., Internet Explorer or Netscape)				
Use a search engine (e.g., Google or Yahoo!)				
Search the Internet for information				
Design a Web page (e.g., using Microsoft FrontPage)				
Use a scanner				
Use a digital camera				
Use a video projector				
Use a handheld computer				

ISTE National Education Technology Standards (NETS) for Students

The NETS for students provide a vision for overall student accomplishment and a set of practical skills and knowledge for students to acquire. Think of the NETS for students as a useful tool in conjunction with your own state standards to help you plan lessons and assess your students. It is imperative to note that technology standards are not designed to be taught in isolation. The technology standards are intended to be learned, practiced, and demonstrated while students are working on content area curriculum. The teacher should insert the technology standards directly into content area lesson plans and develop rubrics using the specific performance indicators. This is not to say that teachers will not need to explicitly teach the technology skills; only that the skills should be taught in conjunction with relevant, meaningful learning experiences as students are problem solving, investigating, and doing research. Let's take a closer look at the NETS for students. The NETS for students are organized into six categories:

- **Basic Operations and Concepts.** These standards address the student's ability to demonstrate proficiency in using technology.

- **Social, Ethical, and Human Issues**. These standards address the student's ability to adhere to the social, ethical, legal, and human issues surrounding technology use in schools.

- **Technology Productivity Tools.** These standards address the student's ability to use technology to produce information in various curriculum areas.

- **Technology Communication Skills.** These standards address the student's ability to use technology to communicate.

- **Technology Research Skills.** These standards address the student's ability to use technology for research.

- **Technology Problem-Solving and Decision-Making Skills.** These standards address the student's ability to use technology to resolve real, authentic problems.

A complete description of the different standards, performance indicators, and performance profiles can be found on the ISTE website. Note that the standards do not list the *specific* skills and knowledge that students should master.

Student Profiles

ISTE developed student profiles to show what a technologically literate student has mastered at the completion of each grade-level range (the grade-level ranges are PreK–2, 3–5, 6–8, and 9–12). The student profiles list the specific performance indicators that students should master. Some examples of the more specific technology skills are as follows. Only a few examples are presented from each of the profile areas. A student who is finishing second grade should be able to use a mouse and keyboard and use the proper vocabulary when sharing about technology. A student who is finishing fifth grade should be able to use technology for writing and select the appropriate technology tools to approach a task. A student who is finishing eighth grade should be able to choose content-specific technology tools for learning and take part in collaborative technology-based research. A student who is finishing 12th grade should be able to make independent decisions about the use of technology and competently use online information.

Get a Clearer Picture of Your Students' Technology Skills

Before you begin planning lessons, it is a good idea to think through the basic computer skills that students need by the end of each grade-level range. Use the appropriate survey from the following pages (depending on your students' grade levels) to gain a clearer picture of what your students can do on a computer. These lists do not include every skill that students should be able to perform, but they include extensive lists that will help you develop a strong idea of your students' levels.

Student Skills Survey

Directions: Estimate the percentage of students in your class that match each particular comfort level for each of the following concepts and/or technologies.

By the end of Grade 2:

Technology Skills:	Can't do this	Can do with assistance	Can do independently	Can teach others
Identify basic hardware components (e.g., monitor, keyboard, mouse, CPU, printer, scanner)				
Understand and use correct computer terminology				
Properly start, restart, and shut down computer				
Identify and know how to use CD and DVD disks				
Properly use mouse; point and click, point and drag, double-click, click from pull-down menu; open and close windows				
Identify icons for files, programs, folders, and disks				
Use the keyboard efficiently: place fingers at the home row and use specific keyboard keys (e.g., space bar, Delete, Return, and arrow keys)				
Identify and use number and letter keys, punctuation and symbol keys, and shift, caps lock, and tab keys				
Use informal keyboarding to enter text				
Use word processing menu options: (e.g., New, Open, Save, Print, and Exit)				
Compose text on a word processor				
Edit text on a word processing document (e.g., change font, font size, font color)				
Save and retrieve text on a word processor				
Add graphic(s) to a word processing document				
Print a word processing document				
Use basic drawing tools in a paint program				
Open and close a program on a CD-ROM				

Student Skills Survey

Directions: Estimate the percentage of students in your class that match each particular comfort level for each of the following concepts and/or technologies.

By the end of Grade 5:

Technology Skills:	Can't do this	Can do with assistance	Can do independently	Can teach others
Type 30 words per minute with 80%–90% accuracy				
Move, resize, and activate an open window				
Copy files to a disk				
Start, use, and close a desk accessory				
Learn formal keyboarding skills for letters and numbers				
Change text by highlighting				
Change font, size, and style of text				
Familiar with word processing menu options (e.g., Cut, Copy, Paste, Undo, Close, Save As, and Print Preview)				
Change page layout (e.g., margins, text alignment)				
Use Spell Check and Thesaurus				
Use Tab key and set and clear tabs				
Print a word processing document				
Master higher functions of creating, changing, and moving graphics using a paint or graphics program				
Change the name of a file				
Choose files to open or delete				
Search files on CD-ROM				
Create folders and organize own data files on computer hard drive or network server				
Create, edit, and save a multimedia file				
Create a series of screens with text, graphics, and navigation buttons				
Present a multimedia project to others				
Use Web browser software				
Use a search engine				
Receive an email, reply to a received email, send a new email, forward an email				
Manage email account using delete/folder options				
Abide by the existing Acceptable Use Policy (AUP)				
Respect the privacy of other students' files				
Understand and respect copyright laws				

Student Skills Survey

Directions: Estimate the percentage of students in your class that match each particular comfort level for each of the following concepts and/or technologies.

By the end of Grade 8:

Technology Skills:	Can't do this	Can do with assistance	Can do independently	Can teach others
Type 35 words per minute with 85%–95% accuracy				
Familiar with additional word processing techniques (e.g., headers and footers, page numbers, word count, page breaks, find/replace command)				
Insert images, objects, and other files into a document				
Familiar with compressing (zip) and uncompressing (unzip) files				
Identify the various file formats that are associated with different applications				
Use utility programs to convert file formats to alternative formats				
Familiar with alternative ways to manage and maintain computer files on different media				
Determine uses of databases and spreadsheets				
Retrieve or edit information in a database				
Perform basic spreadsheet functions				
Select and change information in a spreadsheet cell				
Create, manipulate, and export a graphic from a paint or graphic program to another program				
Upload and download files over the Internet				
Use FTP to transfer files				
Describe the different types of online services				
Familiar with planning and creating a video project				
Use a storyboard				
Create simple animation in a series of screens				
Record or modify sound to add to presentation				
Add an attachment to email				
Evaluate a website for accuracy of information				
Conduct effective and efficient Web searches				
Identify and respect copyright issues on the Web				

Student Skills Survey

Directions: Estimate the percentage of students in your class that match a particular comfort level for each of the following concepts and/or technologies.

By the end of high school:

Technology Skills:	Can't do this	Can do with assistance	Can do independently	Can teach others
Type 40+ words per minute with 90%–100% accuracy				
Master additional word processing menu options (e.g., toolbar and layout menus)				
Master additional word processing techniques (e.g., tables, borders, columns)				
Create a simple database and spreadsheet to store, organize, and sort data				
Use a spreadsheet to answer questions by using formulas and manipulating data				
Generate graphs and charts using data from a spreadsheet				
Identify, evaluate, and fix basic to moderate problems involving hardware, software, and the network				
Use authoring tools to generate Webcasts, videos, Web pages, etc.				
Use appropriate search techniques to minimize unrelated hits				
Create anchors and links within a Web page				
Create pages that load efficiently				
Use bookmarks or favorites to save URLs for later use				

A Reminder About Standards

It is imperative that teachers seek out information on the technology standards and skills required of students in their specific states and districts. As noted above, many states have chosen to use the NETS for students standards. Others have created modified versions of these same standards. Still others may have written their own. Teachers of all grade levels should inquire whether their district or state has set up technology assessments or whether technology is a component of exit exams for any grade level. Technology skills build on one another, and all students are entitled to learn the appropriate skills for their grade levels as they progress in school.

Developing Lessons Using Technology Standards

So now you are faced with two challenges: creating lessons that engage students in worthwhile problems and projects and incorporating technology standards into those lessons. How can you provide lessons incorporating technology standards that require students to do more than regurgitate information or demonstrate a procedure shown to them? How do you create lessons involving technology in which students are engaged in solving problems, answering questions, and completing real-world tasks? Whether you are responsible for teaching the NETS for students, a version of the NETS for students, or a separate set of technology standards, you can incorporate them into engaging lessons that address the academic standards for which you are also responsible. Hawkins (1997) noted that technology-integrated lessons provide access to current primary source material, ways for students and teachers to collaborate with experts from all around the world, and opportunities for extending comprehension through multisense experiences.

How Do Teachers Add Technology Instruction to an Already Full Schedule?

Whenever teachers are confronted with exciting new classroom ideas, the first question is always "How do I fit that in?" There is good news about adding technology to your day. It is not an extra time period of curriculum; rather, technology is incorporated into already existing content lessons. Furthermore, technology often provides the motivation for students to exert their best efforts. The increased motivation deepens retention of content, which can minimize the need to reteach material.

Following are specific content area suggestions for incorporating technology into everyday lessons (Balser, 2001). These ideas are only given to provide a jumpstart of ideas. The possibilities are as endless as your creativity allows.

Math:

- Use spreadsheets to compute mathematical formulas.
- Use spreadsheets to show patterns in math.
- Use graphs to show algebra and trigonometry relations and functions.
- Use email to set up math tutorial relationships among students.

Science:

- Use texts to debate and compare the accuracy of Internet science articles.
- Use spreadsheets to aid in the presentation of data collection.
- Use video microscopes.
- Use simulation software that relates to the given content.
- Analyze data using a computer graphing program.

Language Arts:

- Create multimedia presentations to report relationships between required literatures.

- Use literature databases for research, including any available online or through school districts or local libraries.

- Debate accuracy of Internet articles about a topic of study.

- Use familiar storybooks and literature on CD-ROMs.

- Have students discuss major works of literature with students from other schools, districts, states, or countries via email, discussion boards, or chat rooms.

Social Studies/Geography:

- Use map software to locate areas of study.

- Use Internet to research places and people of study.

- Debate bias in texts and Internet articles.

- Email pen pals in the areas that are being studied.

Ask and Borrow

Here are some ways to develop project-based or problem-based lessons using technology standards. The very best place to start is by talking to fellow teachers who already incorporate technology in meaningful ways into their teaching. Ask them how they manage to address academic standards and technology standards at the same time. See if they have lessons they are willing to share. If the lessons you borrow are not written for your grade level, use them for ideas to develop projects for your own students.

Another excellent way to find tried and true lessons is to search online. The ISTE website provides a searchable lesson database containing lessons and units designed to teach the NETS for students. The lessons in this database are also based on national curriculum standards. Each lesson cites both the NETS standards and the curriculum standards the lesson addresses. Find this page by using a search engine such as Google or Yahoo! and the keywords "NETS lessons" or "ISTE lesson database." Once you find the database, search it by grade level, subject, and/or keywords.

Also search for lessons online in other ways. Use a search engine and keywords that pertain to what you are looking for. For example, if you are a second-grade teacher who wants to incorporate technology into your science lessons, try a search using the keywords "second-grade science lessons technology."

Bit by Bit: Incorporate a Little Technology Into an Existing Lesson

The next best place to start is to take an existing unit or lesson that you have taught before and add a small technology component. Do not feel that you must cover several technology standards at once. In the same vein, do not feel that you must substantially change the lesson or unit. Add a small technology project to the lesson without changing much else. For your very first technology project, try something you feel comfortable showing students. Maybe you have used a word processor like Microsoft Word before. Think of something the students can do with a word processor that will add an interesting, meaningful task to the lesson. For example, for a unit on the Civil War, direct students to compose a letter to a soldier or nurse. It is okay if you are not entirely sure how to use a word processor to do this. You and your students do not need to have mastered all of the technology skills involved in a project before starting. Make use of your students' abilities to figure out how to use new technology. Most likely, some of your students will be familiar with the technology you are introducing. Start by showing the students one or two key technology skills; they can learn the rest while doing the small project. It helps to pair experienced students with less experienced students. They will work together to complete the task.

After you have begun adding small technology components to your lessons, it will become easier to add more. Remember to always strive to make the use of the technology meaningful.

The Possibilities Are Endless

There are exciting things happening all around the nation because teachers are bravely incorporating technology into the curriculum. In Hana, Hawaii, special education students are using special reading computer programs to boost reading skills and their confidence. Speech-to-text software is helping these students express their thoughts about learning when writing can be a physical hardship. The teachers are adapting the programs to meet the individual needs of each of their special education students and seeing remarkable results (Wellington, 1998). Video clubs are also popping up in schools across the nation. They give students a voice and a sense of belonging in a school system where they might not have been succeeding before. Through this technology, students are exploring high interest subjects. Indigenous Choctaw tribal students in Mississippi are sharing poems, tribal history, folklore, and more with other students in the United States and across continents through Internet interactive websites (Ellis, 2002). Students in Spearfish, South Dakota, are holding live video conferences with other students in Sakaide City, Japan (Furger, 2002). The abundance of exciting success stories should be enough to draw teachers into the quest of integrating technology into the classroom. As you gradually add further technology components to additional classroom lessons, you will find yourself meeting more of the technology standards that your district requires. Many districts have curriculum leaders and experts who can offer ideas, equipment, and training. The next chapter will help you by exploring different types of software programs and the types of projects that will help your students succeed in technology.

Chapter Two Reflection

1. What are your reactions to the ISTE National Educational Technology Standards? Explain why you think they either are or are not beneficial to teachers or students.

   _____

   _____

   _____

2. What steps would you take to ensure that you have met the ISTE NETS or your district or state standards for teachers or students?

   _____

   _____

   _____

3. From the list of "Essential Computer Skills for Teachers" (page 36), which five skills do you need to work on most and why?

   _____

   _____

   _____

4. Explain why it is not essential that you or your students have mastered all of the computer skills needed for a project before beginning the project.

   _____

   _____

   _____

Integrate Software Programs Into Your Lessons

You are aware that computers can be excellent tools for learning and you know that there are technology standards that you must teach, but in practical terms, how is this done? The next step is to learn about the abundance of software programs and what they can do for you and your students.

The previous chapters outlined a vision for integrating technology into the classroom. You were introduced to the importance of basing lessons on technology standards. This chapter explores the practical details of using software programs in your lessons. It includes brief descriptions of each software program and straightforward, practical project ideas for using each software program as a tool for learning. Let these project ideas be a springboard to spark ideas for software use in your own classroom.

As you read through Chapter Three, keep in mind that you can use a software program with your students even if you only have minimal experience with it. Choose a single simple task, show the students one or two skills, pair students, and give them a task to complete. As long as they are aware of your expectations for the end product, they will help one another to complete the steps required to accomplish the task.

Before you begin reading Chapter Three, check your knowledge to see how much you know about software programs.

Check Your Knowledge

Directions: Evaluate the accuracy of each statement below. Place a T (for True) or an F (for False) in the space provided.

_____ 1. Each word processing program has its own menu system from which to accomplish the various possible actions.

_____ 2. There are an unlimited number of ideas or ways to integrate word processing into classroom activities.

_____ 3. If you want to create a formatted document, desktop publishing is a completely different process than word processing.

_____ 4. Spreadsheets are only used to manipulate and organize numeric data.

_____ 5. Spreadsheet programs can be used to create word puzzles for vocabulary review.

_____ 6. Students gain problem-solving and critical thinking skills when they learn to use spreadsheet programs.

_____ 7. Due to their degree of difficulty, database programs are limited in how they can be integrated into classroom activities.

_____ 8. Multimedia presentations should be planned on a storyboard prior to using a particular software program.

_____ 9. Rubrics are effective tools for evaluating students' multimedia projects.

_____ 10. Database programs do not lend themselves to developing students' critical thinking skills.

When to Choose a Software Program Over Traditional Classroom Means

There are going to be times when it is not appropriate to use a computer for a classroom task. However, there are also times when the computer is the most obvious tool for creating a dynamic learning experience for students. First, learn about the various options described in this chapter. Challenge yourself to incorporate one component of software for an upcoming unit. Start with a simple project that easily correlates to your curriculum and see where the experience takes your students. David Warlick (2005) states:

> If the students' work can easily be done with pencil and paper, then it should be done with pencil and paper. If their work is to be compiled and published as a school literary magazine, e-mailed to the county commission, or if images or other media are to be integrated into the work, then use a computer. If the information is available in an encyclopedia or other reference book, then use a book. If the information or perspective that you seek is not available in print or if the information is to be processed in some way using a computer, then go to the Internet. When we use technology for teaching or for learning, we should use the technology to take advantage of its unique capabilities. (p. 19)

The most current research shows that these software tools are important for building more knowledge in learning environments. Students use these new technology tools to gather data, organize information, share what they have learned, and demonstrate learning through writing (Norman & Hayden, 2002).

Word Processing

Word processing programs allow students to develop higher-level thinking skills by focusing on composing, creating, and communicating. Also, the features of word processing programs allow students to easily rearrange content and find ways of communicating better. Finally, word processors engage students in the authentic task of publishing more professional-looking documents. Students become more motivated to compose and create when using word processing software (Means et al., 1993).

Word processing programs are the most used software programs in classrooms from elementary grades through high school (Kulik, 2003). The most common word processors are Microsoft Word, WordPerfect, and AppleWorks. Because these programs are so easy to use and have so many functions, they have made the typewriter practically obsolete. In many classrooms, the students opt to use computers rather than pencils (Warlick, 2005). It is now one of the primary ways to put words on paper. Documents can be easily edited before they are printed. An existing document can be used as a template or a model for future documents. This allows the user to edit existing documents rather than to create a new document from scratch each time. This is a major time-saver and provides consistency.

For struggling students, the task of writing is often overwhelming. Having to edit and rewrite an essay can be emotionally and physically demanding on high-needs students, not to mention special education students. The word processing program provides a practical solution. Many struggling students prefer keyboarding their thoughts. Editing does not require crossing words out, ripping the paper with erasures, and rewriting. Students can make changes easily and move on to new writing projects. Linda Yackanicz, from Chestnut Hill College, did her Masters thesis on whether word processing programs are helpful for reluctant writers. Her research found that the use of word processing programs built the confidence of struggling students; they were able to focus on what they were writing, rather than how they were writing. These students actually wrote more, and their writing ability improved significantly (Yackanicz, 2000; Norman & Hayden, 2002). "We know that students write better and learn to write better with a word processor. Writing becomes a craft with this versatile tool" (Warlick, 2005, p. 17).

Word processing can be easily integrated into teaching and learning. It provides the students and teachers the ability to format text, insert and delete text, and copy and paste text. Other features include word wraparound, justification, spell check, and merging. Each word processing program has its own menu system from which to accomplish the various possible actions. Word processing improves the appearance of documents. It saves time and allows users to share information in an electronic format. Students can use word processing to compose stories, write reports, keep notes, and maintain journals related to classroom activities. The following project offers a creative way to use a word processor to enhance student learning. This activity goes beyond the simple task of just typing text from a piece of paper to a computer screen.

Student Project: Publish a Poetry Book (Grades K–2)

One of the simplest ways to use a word processor in a meaningful way is to direct students to create their very own books. Students instantly see the connection between the task and the tool, and they enjoy seeing their books look official, complete with typed text and clip art. Furthermore, composing a book is an excellent way to develop reading, writing, and creative-thinking skills.

Before beginning the lesson, create a document in a word processor with text that the students will complete. Model the text after a book of repetitive text and/or rhyme. For example, for the book *I Went Walking, What Did I See?* by Sue Williams, you could create a page that states: "I went walking. What did I see? I saw a _____ looking at me." Generate three or four pages in the document with the same text. Separate each page by a page break. Be sure to create a title page on the first page in the file. Then, save the document as a read-only file or save it as a template file.

Next, read the book of poetry or repetitive text that correlates with your created document to the students. Ask the students to create more rhymes and have them share with the group. In our example here, for the book *I Went Walking, What Did I See?*, you might request that the students imagine walking through a park. This will focus their creativity as they brainstorm things they might see in the park. Ask students to orally complete the line, "I went walking. What did I see? I saw a _____ looking at me." You can also ask students to imagine walking by the ocean, in the desert, through a castle, through a zoo, or in a museum. Choose a place that relates to something you are studying. Then, ask the students what tools they might use to make a book like the one you just read. Entertain all answers before suggesting that they use the computer to create their very own poetry books. Direct the students to open the document you created and complete the pages by inserting text on each line; they may have to delete the line first in order to enter the name of what they "see." If you wish, have them also insert clip art to illustrate each page. Finally, instruct them to save their documents and print the pages. You might also have them print the pages with only the text and later draw the pictures, depending on how much computer time and access you have.

Figure 3.1: Sample Poetry Book

Excerpted from *Apple Works: Simple Projects (Primary)*. Copyright © 2003 by Teacher Created Materials, Inc.

Desktop Publishing

Desktop publishing programs are advanced versions of word processing programs used for professional and home use alike, thanks to the availability of easy-to-use programs. In the classroom, desktop publishing programs enable students to create products that reflect their understanding of key academic concepts. Students become active constructors of content, which research has shown is greatly superior for learning than passively absorbing content (Roschelle et al., 2001).

The term *desktop publishing* describes the process of laying out and formatting documents to create a more professional look. It uses many of the same processes as word processing for creating formatted documents, but there are many extra features as well. You can use a word processor to desktop publish, but there are also software programs designed specifically for this purpose. These programs allow more control over the design of your page or document. Desktop publishing software provides features like magazine-style columns (for newsletters), rulers, borders and graphics, repeating headers and footers, and a large variety of fonts. Even though word processing programs contain some of these features, page layout programs specialize in making page layout and design easier and more integrated with the text and graphics. Examples of page layout programs are Microsoft Publisher, Print Shop Pro, PageMaker, QuarkXPress, and Adobe InDesign.

Creating documents with desktop publishing software is similar to the procedures of word processing software. Text is typed onto a page and formatted. Images, like pictures and clip art, are inserted later. However, desktop publishing software allows more control over the formatting of documents. You can decide exactly where you want to place text on the page, specify how the text is placed (on top or underneath an image or graphic), and have more control over typographical features like kerning (the space between letters), leading (line spacing), and the presentation of text (making it easy and appealing to read). You can use the mouse to drag and place the elements to the precise location on your created page. With scanners and digital cameras, you can even insert photographs into documents. Desktop publishing also supports a feature called WYSIWYG (pronounced wiz-zee-wig). It stands for "What You See Is What You Get." It means that what you see on your computer screen will look exactly the same way on paper when it is printed. Desktop publishing programs are usually used by intermediate to advanced computer users to create professional quality newsletters, information packets, and more (Norman & Hayden, 2002).

Using Desktop Publishing in the Classroom

As a classroom teacher, you may not always have access to desktop publishing software. Therefore, you may have to use a word processor to complete desktop publishing activities. In most cases, you will probably not even notice the lack of control over text and graphic placement in the word processor. This is due to the improvements in word processing software in recent years.

With access to a desktop publishing program, teachers can use it for professional activities, such as creating lesson plans, seating charts, awards, and certificates. Both teachers and students can use desktop publishing software to make posters about topics studied in class; for example, how to solve a math problem or how to do a science experiment. It can also be used to create ads, banners, cards, report covers, and even personal portfolios. Because the text and images can be so easily manipulated, it is very easy to create a classroom newspaper or newsletter, enhance photos with text, borders, or ruled lines, or create a newspaper about the time period or topic you are studying.

As a jump start to using desktop publishing, two student activities follow. The activities include making an invitation and creating a travel brochure.

Student Project #1: You're Invited! (Grades 3–5)

In this activity, the students create a quarter-fold (or half-fold) invitation for a particular event or topic that they are studying in class. For example, the invitation could invite spectators to attend the signing of the Declaration of Independence. Creating an invitation to an historical event connects the students to the actual event and the historical figures. Students involve themselves in history and history becomes more real to them. Plus, creating the invitation involves research and critical thinking about the audience and the purpose of the invitation.

Before beginning the lesson, discuss the historical event, its context, and its importance in history. For example, for the Declaration of Independence signing, discuss the people involved, their motivations and anxieties, and the political and economic issues of the time. Tell the students to imagine that they are the people who organized the event. Ask them why they are holding the event and who it might be important to invite. Then, tell the students that they will be researching the event further and creating an invitation for the event.

Direct the students to research the event with specific purposes in mind: the date(s), where it took place, who was there, who organized the event, and why the event was planned. Allow the students to use multiple resources, including books and the Internet (see Chapter Four for more information on how to help your students conduct research using the Internet). Next, direct the students to complete the activity using either desktop publishing software or word processing software. While desktop publishing software is actually the best to use because it offers more flexibility, word processing software will also meet your needs, if necessary. Tell the students to include all the important pieces of information that you asked them to find in the final product. Invite them to be creative with the invitation. Figure 3.2a shows a sample cover for Thomas Jefferson's invitation. Figure 3.2b shows a sample inside of the invitation.

Figure 3.2a: Sample Invitation Cover

Figure 3.2b: Sample Inside of Invitation

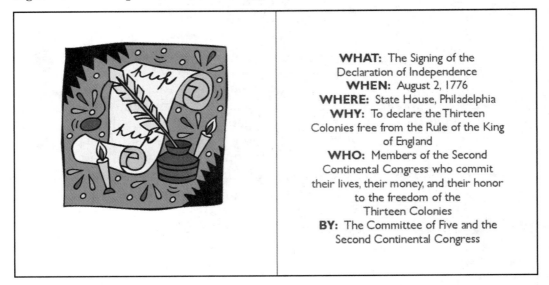

WHAT: The Signing of the Declaration of Independence
WHEN: August 2, 1776
WHERE: State House, Philadelphia
WHY: To declare the Thirteen Colonies free from the Rule of the King of England
WHO: Members of the Second Continental Congress who commit their lives, their money, and their honor to the freedom of the Thirteen Colonies
BY: The Committee of Five and the Second Continental Congress

Student Project #2: Traveling Through History (Grades 3–5 and 6–8)

For this project, students will research a place from a certain time period and then create a travel brochure to showcase the information. This project will help students develop higher-order thinking skills by researching, synthesizing information, and representing what they have learned. According to experts in technology integration, this type of project, with students aided by technology to create a polished product, will facilitate deeper learning (Means et al., 1993).

To begin, direct the students to research a place in history that ties into what you are studying. Ask them to find key pieces of information, such as where the place is on a map, dates of the era, the language and customs of the people living there, the highlights of the landscape (e.g., special geological formations, bodies of water, etc.), and forms of entertainment or special events. For example, students might research a medieval city in Europe.

When students have finished their research, create a model of a completed project so that they can see what is expected and what possibilities the program allows. Then direct them to use a desktop publishing program or word processing program to create their own brochures. Allow the students to show their brochures to the rest of the class when they are completed. You might ask them to pretend to be travel agents and to use their brochures to entice others to visit the place they are showcasing.

Figures 3.3a and 3.3b shows a sample brochure created to entice travelers to explore life during medieval times. When both documents are printed back-to-back, they become a tri-fold brochure.

Figure 3.3a: Brochure Sample 1

WHERE YOUR JOURNEY WILL TAKE YOU

Medieval Europe covered a large area. Walled cities, or boroughs, were found scattered all over Europe, from Italy to Germany.

Our tour will take you to one walled city that time forgot. Experience the actual daily life and festivals of medieval city dwellers!

FOR MORE INFORMATION

Please contact Medieval Tours, Inc. today to sign up for the adventure of a lifetime!

Medieval Tours, Inc.

One Borough Way
Medieval City, Europe
87654

Phone: 555-555-5555
Fax: 555-555-5555
E-mail: someone@medieval.com

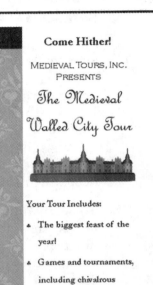

Come Hither!

MEDIEVAL TOURS, INC.
PRESENTS

The Medieval Walled City Tour

Your Tour Includes:

- The biggest feast of the year!
- Games and tournaments, including chivalrous jousting!
- Tours of walled cities and authentic medieval dwellings and castles!

MEDIEVAL TOURS, INC.

Figure 3.3b: Brochure Sample 2

THE MEDIEVAL BOROUGH:
'TIS MOST SPLENDID!

Walled City Life

Come see how the medieval bourgeoisie really lived. Witness firsthand how the lives of walled city dwellers were tied to the harvests and the castle lord from 500 A.D. to 1500 A.D.

A MAIDEN'S HAT

Imagine yourself a medieval city dweller protected by the walls from Viking invaders!

Feasts

Medieval festivals were tied to feasts that marked important harvesting days in the year. Come join in on the biggest feast of the year which began on Christmas Eve and ended on

MEAT FROM THE "BLOOD MONTH"

January 6th. During this time gorge youself on food provided by the castle lord.

Games and Tournaments

Medieval city dwellers spent much of their time working. There was much to do to meet the daily requirements of food, shelter, and clothing. However, occasionally there was time for games, and on your tour of a walled city, you can play chess, dice games, bowling, checkers, and backgammon.

A CHESS SET

You may also watch the tournaments provided by the castle lord. Knights will amaze you with their

A KNIGHT SERVING HIS CASTLE LORD

jousting skills and fighting prowess.

Landscape and Buildings

Come see how medieval city dwellers built their homes of stone. You'll be amazed how poorer families lived together in just one room while wealthier families occupied entire structures. Imagine how difficult it was to keep out the cold and to see inside these dark quarters. Sit on the same wooden benches that medieval people sat on while they ate their meals!

Admire the beautiful countryside surrounding the borough. Notice how much of the countryside is used for farming and grazing animals.

Tour the castles of the village and city lords and imagine how luxurious these cold, damp castles

A MEDIEVAL CASTLE

must have seemed to the villagers and the bourgeoisie.

Spreadsheet Programs

Spreadsheets are effective tools in both teaching and learning. While mostly used for math, they are also widely used for science, social studies, and language arts. Through the use of spreadsheets, students can experiment with variables to change equations or tables. They can organize data that can be instantly converted by the computer into a variety of graphs. They also help students to manipulate, analyze, and reflect on collected data (Norman & Hayden, 2002). Spreadsheets are very powerful tools that allow students to understand complicated word problems. They can be used to teach students techniques in problem solving by posing and answering "what if" questions. Spreadsheets teach students how to think at a higher level in order to solve real-life word problems.

Instead of using calculators or calculating by hand, use spreadsheet programs to make processing calculations faster and more accurate. A spreadsheet application allows you to manipulate and organize numbers in various documents, such as personal budgets, financial statements, grade sheets, and sales records. It can perform simple or complex calculations involving the numbers that you have entered into the columns and rows. The program easily performs mathematical functions across columns and rows, such as addition, subtraction, division, and multiplication, as well as averages and means. The data can be in the form of labels, values, and formulas. The advantages of using a spreadsheet are that it can use formulas to calculate data, automatically update values when they are related to data being changed, and display data in graphs and charts. All information is contained in precise cells, labeled by column and row number.

Sometimes, it is optimal to use a spreadsheet instead of a word processing program because you do not have to struggle with tab stops to line up columns of information. There are several different spreadsheet programs available. Microsoft Excel, Lotus 1-2-3, Quattro Pro, and AppleWorks are just a few examples. Regardless of which program you use, there are some standard components to all spreadsheet programs. Each spreadsheet file is called a *workbook*. Each workbook can hold several activity sheets. A *worksheet* is the grid of columns and rows where all of the information is manipulated. Each worksheet consists of an almost unlimited number of cells. Each *cell* is the intersection of a column and row within the worksheet. The user can easily change the width and height of each column and row to contain the amount of numerical or word information desired.

Using a Spreadsheet in the Classroom

Because every teacher is required to manage student and classroom data in some way, spreadsheet programs have the capability of being an integral part of teacher productivity (Fryer, 2001). While word processing software can certainly streamline the creation and management of text documents, a spreadsheet offers advantages over word processors that should not be overlooked. Usually teachers use spreadsheet programs to keep accurate, organized records of grades, classroom budgets, attendance, and checklists. However, they can also be used to generate lesson plan templates, to create word search and crossword puzzles, and to create seating charts.

When students use spreadsheet programs to manipulate data related to classroom studies, they build analytical skills, mathematical skills, interpretive skills and, of course, technical skills. Research shows that when students use computers in science labs to graph the results of science experiments, students' learning is greatly enhanced (Roschelle et al., 2001). Even if you do not have computers in your school science lab, you can still draw enormous benefit by having your students use spreadsheet programs to manipulate data. Even very young students can collect data and create pie charts, line graphs, and bar graphs. As you know, most state content standards require that students learn to create, read, and interpret these types of graphs.

There are multitudes of ways in which to integrate spreadsheet activities into classroom activities. Teachers can use them to keep student grades, monitor student reading logs, and even maintain a classroom budget. Students can use spreadsheets to predict changes in numbers, build different kinds of graphs, and conduct and record class surveys.

A specific example of a project that incorporates spreadsheet software is described below.

Student Project: How Healthy Is Fast Food? (Grades 6–8 and 9–12)

In this activity, the students compare and evaluate the nutritional information of different foods from multiple fast-food restaurants. Before the students start this project, you or the students should obtain nutritional information from fast-food restaurants or from their websites. Also, find the United States Department of Agriculture (USDA) recommended calorie intake appropriate for the genders, ages, and heights of the students in your classroom.

To start the activity, tell students that they will be on vacation for a week and will only have access to fast-food restaurants. Using either their prior knowledge of fast-food restaurants and menus, actual menus brought in for the assignment, or Internet-researched menus as a resource, they must write down what they would eat for three daily meals for the entire week. Older students should record actual sizes in ounces; younger students should record sizes in small, medium, or large and record data for a shorter period of time than that of the older students. Direct students to then create a spreadsheet that will display the nutritional information for different fast foods. The spreadsheet should list the type of food, the restaurant from which it came, and its nutritional information. Figure 3.4 shows a possible setup of one lunch meal for students in grades 6–8. Figure 3.5 shows an expanded example that would be appropriate for students in grades 9–12. The assignment can be adapted for whatever analytical use the teacher has planned for the learning experience. Using the nutritional information from the fast-food restaurants, students should insert the appropriate information for each column. Teach the students how to use automatic sum feature in order to compile the total for each column.

Figure 3.4: Fast Food Spreadsheet Sample (Grades 6–8)

	A	B	C	D	E	
1		Calories	Fat Calories	Non-fat Calories	Percentage of Fat	
2	Cheeseburger					
3	Large Fries					
4	Apple Pie					
5	Diet Coke					
6	Total					
7						

Figure 3.5: Fast Food Spreadsheet Sample (Grades 9–12)

	A	B	C	D	E	F	G	H	
1	Restaurant 1	Size	Calories	Calories from fat	Total Fat (g)	Sodium	Carbs	Dietary Fiber	
2	Cheeseburger								
3	French Fries								
4	Diet Coke								
5	Apple Pie								
6	Total:								
7									

As an extension activity, instruct the students to create another spreadsheet. On this worksheet, the students need to compute and transfer each day's fast-food calorie intake and compare it to the USDA recommended calorie intake. Figure 3.6 shows how this spreadsheet might look.

Figure 3.6: Calorie Intake Spreadsheet

	A	B	C	
1	Day:	My Calorie Intake	Recommended Calorie Intake	
2	Sunday			
3	Monday			
4	Tuesday			
5	Wednesday			
6	Thursday			
7	Friday			
8	Saturday			
9				

For the last part of the activity, students can return to the nutritional information sheets and plan a new weekly menu, using the previously created spreadsheets. This time, the students must stay within the guidelines of their recommended daily calorie intake while eating at the same fast-food restaurants. As a class, discuss how a person can splurge or treat oneself to a high-calorie item but still stay within the recommended daily calorie intake. The students will become quite creative!

Databases

A database program provides a way to collect and organize large amounts of information. It is also referred to as an electronic filing system. Electronic catalog systems in libraries are examples of commonly used databases in schools. Catalog systems allow you to retrieve information about publications in the library. For example, you can enter an author's name, and only books from that author will be displayed. In addition to electronic catalog systems, other examples of everyday databases include electronic address books, grocery store inventories, and music file lists in a media player. There are many practical ways for students to use databases. Students can use commercial databases and information services to conduct research on weather and science data (Norman & Hayden, 2002).

Creating and using a database requires students to gather and organize data into sets (or records) and to manipulate this data to discover patterns and trends among the entries. Creating a database places the student in an active role where he/she collects and organizes what appears to be unrelated information into meaningful categories. Students are then responsible for analyzing, synthesizing, and evaluating this information. When older students use databases to record data from scientific experiments or even statistical data from social studies research, they can find relationships and test variables in complex systems (Means et al., 1993). There are a number of different database programs available for teachers and students. Microsoft Access, AppleWorks, and FileMaker Pro are just a few.

A Brief Overview of How to Use a Database

The most important thing to do when you start creating a database is to think ahead. Before you turn on the computer, think about the type of information that you want to collect and how you will use this information later. For example, in a database of student information, you will want contact information to be available at a click of the mouse. You will want to collect the name, address, and phone number of each student, plus other details such as birth date, parents' names, parents' work phone numbers, and the name and phone number of an emergency contact.

As you look over the list, it seems to be complete. However, what happens if you decide to print a class list sorted alphabetically by the students' last names? There is no easy way to do it, so it makes sense to break the field "Name" into "Last name" and "First name." Do the same thing with the student's address, parents' names and work numbers, and the emergency contact name and number. It is crucial to assign each information category its own field so that you will later be able to sort the database using that particular field. The revised fields will be similar to the following:

- Student's first name
- Student's last name
- Street address
- City
- Zip code

- Home phone number
- Birth date
- Father's first name
- Father's last name
- Mother's first name
- Mother's last name
- Father's work phone number
- Mother's work phone number
- Emergency contact's first name
- Emergency contact's last name
- Emergency contact's phone number

After you have determined which fields to use, enter several details about the fields that you are using. Some of the information that the database program requires is the particular field that each key is in (i.e., the primary field used for sorting), the size of the field (i.e., how many characters the field can hold), and what kind of information the field will hold (i.e., if it will hold numbers, values, or text).

Once all of the fields and records have been stored, it is time for the database file to be put to work. The main job of a database is to provide answers to questions. In fact, one of the major components of most databases is a query tool—a special feature that lets you ask questions (queries) that will elicit useful answers from the stored data. For example, in the previously mentioned database of student information, you might want to know which students have birthdays in March. You could sort the data by last name and birth date. The database file answers your question by creating a query or sorting the records and displaying only the ones that meet your specified criteria. In addition, you can easily create forms in which you can enter, update, or display the data.

Using Databases in the Classroom

In a science or health class, the students can generate a database of nutritional information from fast-food restaurants. After all of the information has been entered into the database file, the students can then begin to build comparisons. The students might ask the following questions:

- Which combo meal has the most calories?
- Which burger has the most grams of fat?
- How many carbohydrates are in a large container of french fries?

Throughout this activity, the students are asking questions, retrieving answers, and analyzing and evaluating the results. In this way, using database programs helps the students to improve their problem-solving and critical thinking skills.

There are additional ways to integrate database programs into the classroom. Some of them include collecting data on a topic being studied in class, like the Periodic Table, presidents, and planets. The students can also use database programs to collect sports data, to maintain lists of books for recreational reading, to store facts about famous people or events, or to collect scientific data. Databases can also be used by teachers to write form letters for parent/teacher communication, maintain a classroom inventory, maintain a student directory, and record and organize discipline referrals or classroom behavior of students.

The following project offers an example of how database programs can be effectively integrated into the classroom.

Student Project: Literature Critics (Grades 3–5 and 6–8)

This project involves gathering information about different types of literature and compiling the information into a classroom database. Throughout the school year, the students can continually add factual information, as well as their opinions, about the different books, stories, and poems that they have read.

The database should consist of a number of headings that reflect the type of information that you want the students to enter. You should create the database for younger students, but for older students, select two or three students to work on it when they have extra class time. Sample headings may include Student Name, Book Title, Author, Publisher, Copyright Date, Genre (e.g., Biography, Mystery, Science Fiction), Main Character(s), Setting, Plot, Rating (1–10), Recommend? (Yes/No), and Student Critique.

As the students finish reading their own books or a book assigned by the teacher, instruct them to enter the information about the book into the database file. Once the information for approximately 20 books has been entered, the students can begin to analyze the different records in the database. For example, students can create a list of all of the mystery books the class has read or of all of the books rated above a five. After printing a list, students can meet to discuss and compare books and make connections between them. They can discuss different genres, expand on their critiques, explain how they assigned a rating, and explain why they decided to recommend or not recommend a particular book. They can also print all of their critiques and see how they have made progress in critiquing books over time.

Figure 3.7: Sample Database

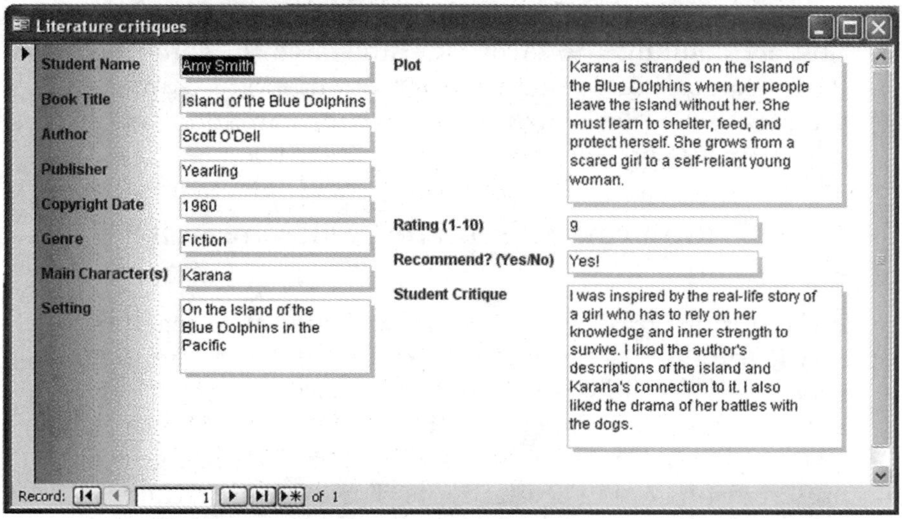

Multimedia Presentation Software

Remember that in the educational setting, technology helps teachers shift from the role of teacher as lecturer to teacher as coach (Graham & Mason, 2000). Presentation software makes it possible for teachers and students to share ideas and communicate through multimedia. Multimedia software programs enable not only teachers but also students to demonstrate, illustrate, and clarify information through the use of technology. Students can construct and represent content that they have gathered, analyzed, and synthesized to create an exciting visual presentation. As an added benefit, students enjoy using multimedia presentation software because they can create a polished, colorful, and animated presentation complete with sound and graphics. Multimedia is becoming the chosen media of our students. "We grew up where information was best delivered on paper. Our children, on the other hand, are growing in a world with not only pictures and words but where video and sound abound and where increasingly we interact with the information that surrounds us in ways that put us in control of knowledge" (Warlick, 2005, p. 17). Multimedia is a term that means that text, graphics, sound, video, and animation are combined to create an integrated presentation. PowerPoint, HyperStudio, Kid Pix, and Harvard Graphics are a few examples of applications that can help to create a multimedia presentation.

Using Multimedia Presentation Software in the Classroom

Presentation software can be incorporated into teaching and learning in a number of ways. The most common way is for individuals or groups to create presentations. Both teachers and students (either individually or cooperatively) can use presentation software to create engaging presentations on a specific topic. For example, students might share the results of extensive research projects by creating and presenting Microsoft PowerPoint shows to their class. As the teacher, you can use multimedia software to present entire lessons. Some districts have purchased the extra equipment to display the computer screen image onto a large classroom screen for easier visibility. Presenting a lesson in this way offers both a visual guide and a tool for reinforcing the main points of the lesson.

As a classroom teacher, it is extremely important to create an instructional plan before you start a multimedia project with students. Make sure that you have a clear purpose and a clear way to evaluate the students' final projects. There are a number of things to consider as you begin to plan your multimedia project.

First of all, it is very important to create a storyboard before using the software. The students draw each slide or scene in the squares of a large grid (6–8 squares on one piece of paper) in order to correctly sequence the project. Depending on the number of slides in the presentation, each student could end up using several sheets of paper.

The second step is to determine if the students are to work individually or in small groups. It is also important to decide how the software will be used to help you teach your curriculum. Direct the students to research a topic related to what you are studying and then create a presentation using the information they gathered.

The third step is to determine what software to use. If the school has a variety of multimedia software programs, it is important to determine whether the students may individually choose the software program they want to use or if all of the students must use the same program. If the students are permitted to choose their own programs, you must also make sure that there are enough computers and/or software licenses for the specific programs that the students want to use. Furthermore, if the students choose different programs, you should also be familiar with all of the programs to help the students with their projects.

The fourth step is to consider computer access. A multimedia project can require a great deal of computer time, depending on the students' skill levels and the project requirements. Therefore, determine if the classroom computers will meet your students' needs or if the computer lab must be reserved to provide extra computer time.

The last step in creating a multimedia project is to determine what you expect from students when their projects are done. By presenting students with clear project directions and a rubric that defines the expectations of the completed project, you can provide them with all of the necessary information to create a successful multimedia project.

It is very important to discuss with the students the dos and the don'ts of creating a multimedia presentation. According to Teachnology (2006), it is important to coach the students to refrain from having "overzealous concentration on the utilization of PowerPoint, while concurrently disregarding the content being exhibited" (What's All the Hype? section, para. 5). Students might get so eager about placing sounds, clip art, and animation into their presentations that they forget to focus on the content guiding the presentation. By modeling appropriate examples and carefully monitoring student creative processes, teachers can emphasize that the content of the presentation is much more important than all of the "bells and whistles" that are added to the slides or cards through the text, graphics, and backgrounds.

There are multiple ways in which to incorporate multimedia projects into the classroom. Students can use them to present research reports or book reports, create a portfolio, or to explain certain content area concepts to their peers. For example, students can use multimedia software to explain the various steps involved to solve an equation in math class, present information about a famous ruler or facts about a specific country in social studies class, explain how the digestive system works in science class, or give a persuasive speech in English class. Below is one detailed project that will hopefully spark additional ideas as to how to integrate multimedia projects into the classroom.

Student Project: Disneyland in Space (Grades 3–5)

Tell students that Disneyland has decided to offer something exciting to its visitors—a new Disneyland park located on another planet. The problem is that Disney does not know which planet is the best one for the new park. Disneyland needs the students' help. The challenge for each student is to figure out which planet among three choices (Uranus, Saturn, and Jupiter) is the best location for the new park and to create a persuasive presentation that will convince the Disney executives of the findings. Note that this project follows Jamie McKenzie's (2000) methodology of conducting research, analyzing the data, synthesizing the data, and constructing a real-life presentation. Not only are students conducting research and learning about the planets, but they must apply the research in a meaningful way.

The teacher should monitor the students as they conduct their research of the three planets. The students should research the distance to each planet, the surface features, climate, and temperatures of each planet, the availability of water on each planet, and interesting places on each planet (i.e., potential locations for the park). Be sure to explain that fuel is expensive and that they should consider this when researching the distance to each planet.

In their presentations, the students must each present the challenge of the project, describe each planet, and present their choice of planet and the reasons why it is the best location for a new Disneyland park. Figures 3.8a–c show some sample template slides you could present to the class in PowerPoint that they will need to fill in with the information for their presentations. These sample templates correspond to the slides on which students would present the project challenge and the introductory information for the first planet. Figures 3.9a–c show how the same slides might look when they are completed by the students.

Before beginning the project, develop a rubric explaining your expectations and present this to the students (see Figure 5.1 for a sample rubric). Providing students with a rubric before starting a project helps them clearly understand the expectations for the project and how these expectations are guidelines for determining the extent to which they are successful with the project. Also, before students create their presentations, have them create storyboards of their presentations.

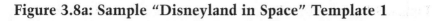

Figure 3.8a: Sample "Disneyland in Space" Template 1

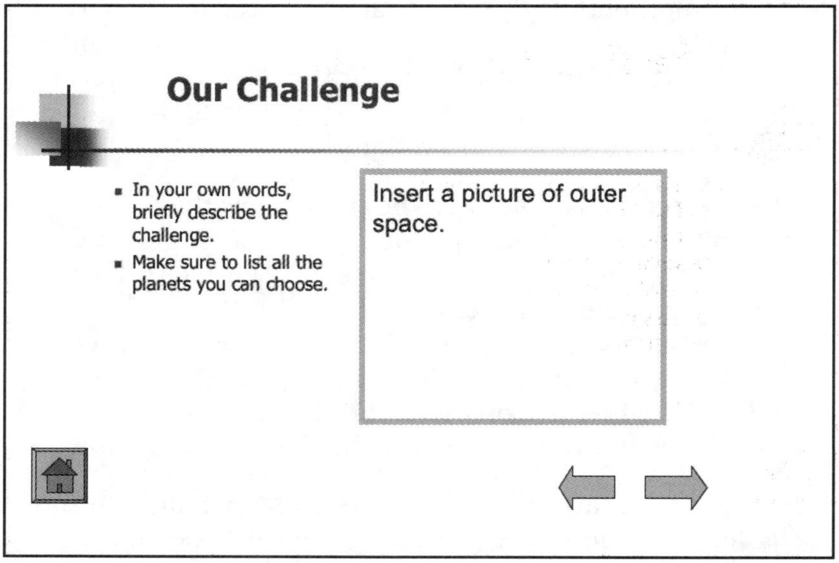

Our Challenge

- In your own words, briefly describe the challenge.
- Make sure to list all the planets you can choose.

Insert a picture of outer space.

Figure 3.8b: Sample "Disneyland in Space" Template 2

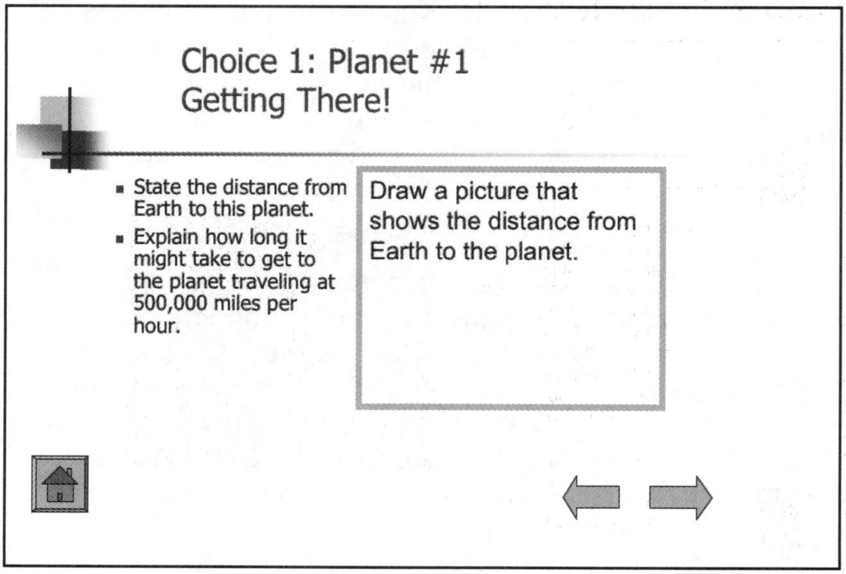

Choice 1: Planet #1
Getting There!

- State the distance from Earth to this planet.
- Explain how long it might take to get to the planet traveling at 500,000 miles per hour.

Draw a picture that shows the distance from Earth to the planet.

Excerpted from *TechTools: Resource Kit for Microsoft PowerPoint.* Copyright © 2003 by Teacher Created Materials, Inc.

Figure 3.8c: Sample "Disneyland in Space" Template 3

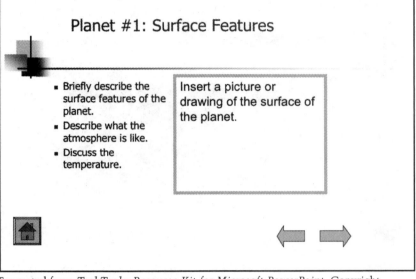

Excerpted from *TechTools: Resource Kit for Microsoft PowerPoint.* Copyright © 2003 by Teacher Created Materials, Inc.

Figure 3.9b: Sample Completed Template 2

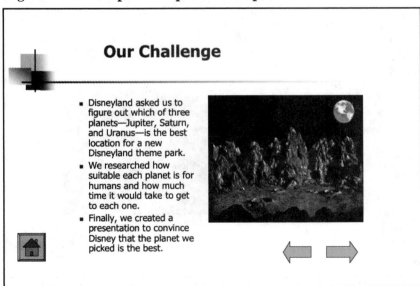

Image from Clipart.com

Figure 3.9b: Sample Completed Template 2

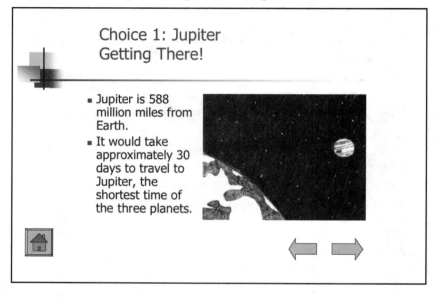

Figure 3.9c: Sample Completed Template 3

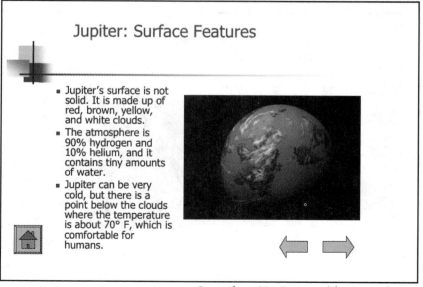

Image from J.L. Gutierrez/Shutterstock, Inc.

As you can see, there are many ways to incorporate software programs into the classroom in meaningful ways. The most important consideration is whether or not students are using software programs to express themselves, apply knowledge, create meaningful products, communicate, or construct content related to the curriculum.

The Long-Term Effects of Using Software in the Classroom

Research shows that not only are teachers better prepared than ever to use software in the classroom, but also that students are increasingly using computers as tools with these types of described software programs, rather than preset tutor programs (Kulik, 2003). What are the long-term effects of using software in the classroom? Recent studies show that instructional technology is thriving today, as both teachers and students are more computer-literate and computers are faster, friendlier, and more accessible in schools (Kulik). All the described projects in this chapter have demonstrated that these types of programs allow students to use higher-level thinking skills. Students tend to exhibit an increase in their abilities to write well, a better understanding of mathematics skills, greater problem-solving skills, better critical thinking skills, and more confidence in the ability to use computers. One study shows that when students are given clear expectations, are assessed in an ongoing manner, and have the opportunity for peer feedback, then they become more engaged learners who are responsible for their own learning, show high levels of motivation for their course projects, and display evidence of strategic thought in planning and executing their projects (McKenzie, 1998).

Chapter Three Reflection

1. After reviewing the capabilities of word processing, database, spreadsheet, multimedia, and desktop publishing software programs, explain how they can assist a teacher in being more productive.

   _____

   _____

   _____

2. Explain how the use of software encourages higher-level thinking skills (such as to analyze, evaluate, and synthesize) in student tasks.

   _____

   _____

   _____

3. How will integrating software programs into your lessons affect the curriculum?

   _____

   _____

   _____

4. Think of a unit of study you currently teach. How could you use one of these software programs within the unit?

   _____

   _____

   _____

Use the Internet to Teach Information Literacy

The Internet has introduced computer users to easy access of valuable information and a multitude of helpful resources. However, on the flip side, some might argue that it provides *too much* information, or "info-glut" (McKenzie, 2000). As availability grows every day, students have access to global information anytime, anyplace; they can even access the Internet on their telephones (Warlick, 2005). The National Center for Education Statistics (NCES) has used its Fast Response Survey System (FRSS) to track access to technology in schools and classrooms since 1994. They found in Fall 2003 that nearly 100 percent of public schools in the United States had access to the Internet, compared with

35 percent in 1994 (Parsad & Jones, 2005). With a simple search, you can find thousands of websites on just about any topic you care to research. On the other hand, some of these websites will undoubtedly be of questionable quality or accuracy. Because of the volume of information and the potential for encountering fraud, teachers and students must develop important searching and critical thinking skills when using the Internet. Teachers and students must learn to sift through the "info-glut" and find the information they seek. This is a learned skill which requires its own set of higher-order thinking skills. They must learn to be critical of what they read and also learn how to apply what is useful. Teachers and students who can do this are information literate.

In addition, the Internet is a powerful communication tool. Students can develop important communication skills for now and the future by using tools such as email, chat rooms, discussion boards, listservs, and instant messaging. However, students must be taught to use these tools wisely. It is well known that students are vulnerable to fraud and malicious intent when participating in online conversations. Equip your students to see beyond the words on the Web page. Help them to develop important critical thinking skills that will protect them and enable them to make the most of the Internet. Help your students become information literate.

The focus of this chapter is to provide teachers with suggestions and ideas for how to use and evaluate the Internet's resources and how to integrate the Internet into lessons so that students can harness the power of the Internet for productive purposes.

Before continuing this chapter, check your knowledge to see how familiar you are with the Internet and communication using Internet technology.

Check Your Knowledge

Directions: Evaluate the accuracy of each statement below. Place a T (for True) or an F (for False) in the space provided.

_____ 1. To be information literate is to know how to navigate the Internet.

_____ 2. Placing quotation marks around a phrase when searching will help to narrow the search results.

_____ 3. The URL (Uniform Resource Locator) can help to determine the authenticity of a website.

_____ 4. When you do an Internet search and get 4,500 hits (results), the 3,000th hit is just as important as the fifth hit.

_____ 5. The Internet should be used as a resource for every student research project.

_____ 6. A hotlist is a list of links set up by the teacher to direct students in a classroom project.

_____ 7. A WebQuest is another term for surfing the Internet.

_____ 8. Internet Exchange Projects involve the collaboration of two or more classrooms that use the Internet to share project-based information.

_____ 9. Weblogs are for posting personal opinions and offer no real educational benefit.

_____ 10. There are search engines that are kid-friendly.

Information Literacy

Chapter One noted that an information literate student is able to question, think independently, invent, research, and problem solve. What does this mean in the context of the Internet? As stated above, the Internet can overload us with information. It has provided schools with "unprecedented access to information in its vastness, convenience, media formats, variety of perspectives, and opportunities for interactivity" (Warlick, 2005, p. 17). The sheer volume of information requires new approaches and even sharper critical thinking skills. And sometimes this information is unreliable and even fraudulent.

More than ever before in history, students must become information literate in order to succeed in school and beyond. Dr. M. Ellen Jay, the 1999–2000 president of the American Association of School Librarians (AASL) says, "There is no textbook for life, and schools can no longer define success in terms of student learning of a predetermined set of facts. Schools need to educate students to cope with a future of constantly changing needs and information" (Jay, 2006, para. 6).

In addition to information literacy, many researchers and educators are now considering other literacies, which are all closely tied to the role of the media and technologies in students' education. Among these other literacies is media literacy, which Renee Hobbs (2006) notes is "the centrality of 'composition' using media tools and technologies . . . [M]edia literacy practices involve students in actively creating messages using publishing software, digital cameras, video, and other media" (p. 18). There is clearly a very fine line between the defining characteristics of information literacy and media literacy. As more states begin to implement media literacy standards, distinctions between information literacy and media literacy will become more and more prominent.

So, how do we help students use the Internet, among other resources, to find, evaluate, and apply information? How do we teach them to carefully investigate and then draw new conclusions, rather than simply collect information on a shallow topic and then regurgitate it into a report? This is a tall order. Students today may be skilled at navigating the Internet, but they may not be wise investigators of information.

This chapter will provide further insight into information literacy by outlining some of the processes, projects, and skills you can use or develop in your classroom by using the Internet as a tool for learning.

What Does the Internet Offer to Classroom Research?

David Warlick (2005) discusses why a teacher would even want to use the Internet in the classroom. He suggests that the use of the Internet invites collaboration: "Internet tools provide links between people, links that unfold within contexts of our professional and personal goals. Within these online collaborations and resulting virtual communities, people tend to accomplish things that are bigger than any one of them" (p. 34). While students often personally invite collaboration through email, video games linked up to other computers, and instant messaging, they can invite collaboration in research through other means. For example, Warlick explains that websites are a close tie to the author; students can also use different software for the different purposes involved in the whole research project, i.e., word processing software for reporting and presentation software for visually presenting research; and finally, web-based services offer observation of similarities and differences between various authors on the same subject matter. Furthermore, the information on the Internet can be more current than available library books. Teachers should direct students to check when the site was last updated. The Internet provides access to multiple perspectives, opinions, and views on a single topic.

The Research Cycle

An excellent way to develop information literacy skills is to direct students in a research project. However, simply handing students a topic and telling them to find information on that topic may result in disorganized and shallow work. The students might simply find information on the topic without any real interest in the topic. They will most likely try to hobble together facts and other people's opinions into some kind of report. This process will not develop higher-order thinking skills and will not engage students in learning.

So, how do you structure a research project that will interest students, teach them information literacy skills, and enable them to draw their own conclusions and create persuasive presentations? By no means is this process Internet-exclusive. As a matter of fact, sometimes the Internet may not be the best resource for students to use. However, many times it will be, and that is why this process is described in this chapter.

Technology integration expert Jamie McKenzie advocates that students be taught to investigate questions by following a research cycle. The steps of McKenzie's research cycle are: Questioning, Planning, Gathering, Sorting and Sifting, Synthesizing, Evaluating, and Reporting (McKenzie, 2000). Each of these processes needs extensive teacher modeling and vigilant monitoring of students' computer use.

- **Questioning**—The students should spend ample time defining the central question of their research to formulate a question that emphasizes a problem or decision. Then, they should brainstorm related questions to guide their research.

- **Planning**—The students should brainstorm the best ways to find the information they seek. They must think about where to find the most reliable and pertinent information.

- **Gathering**—The students should use the identified resources to gather only relevant and useful information. If the Internet is not identified as the best information source for a topic, then students should not use it.

- **Sorting and Sifting**—The students should sort and sift through the information and identify and organize only those pieces that will lead to further insight into the question or problem at hand.

- **Synthesizing**—The students should consider the pieces of information identified during sorting and sifting and try to find relationships and patterns. This process will lead them to new insight.

- **Evaluating**—The students should evaluate what they have found and concluded and decide if more information is needed.

- **Reporting**—The students may go through the research cycle many times before proceeding to this final step. Now the students report their findings and recommendations. They may create persuasive presentations using presentation software.

Searching the Internet

There will be many times when the Internet is the best resource for finding relevant information. Both teachers and students need to learn how to use it wisely. But, how can you possibly search the Internet with any accuracy when it is so vast? While most experts propose that it is impossible to precisely pinpoint the absolute size of the entire Internet, it is estimated that the Internet is composed of millions, or even billions, of Web pages. Here we will outline some ways to search the Internet effectively, accurately, and wisely.

There are a number of things that you can do to help make an Internet search more effective. First, use a search engine. Search engines "are information assistants who aid you in finding the information that you need to solve a problem, answer a question, or make a decision" (Warlick, 2005, p. 126). A search engine uses keywords or terms that you enter to search through millions of websites. Examples of search engines include Google, Yahoo!, Ask.com, and Dogpile. Start by typing in very specific search terms. This will help you get a few hundred results rather than millions of results. Each search engine usually only displays up to 20 results at a time. Other search tips:

- Make sure that all keywords and words in the search phrases are spelled correctly.

- Uppercase and lowercase letters generally have no effect on your search.

- Do the same search using different search engines or directories.

- Substitute keywords with appropriate synonyms for alternate searches.

- Keep track of words or phrases that are generated from your current search. Often, these keywords can be used in additional searches and generate new results that are helpful.

There are also many kid-friendly search engines. They tend to limit the search results to age-appropriate sites. Some search engines even have educators verify the accuracy and appropriateness of websites that are accessed during the searches. Some examples of kid-friendly search engines include Ask For Kids, KidsClick,

Yahooligans!, and CyberSleuth Kids (see Appendix A for specific links to these and other kid-friendly search engines).

Knowing how to use quotation marks is also very important. Quotes are not needed when searching with one keyword. If you are searching for information about elephants, you would enter the word *elephant* or *elephants* in the search box and click the Search button. However, if you are using multiple words or a phrase to search for information on the Internet, you will want to use quotes around all the words. This will cause the search engine to search for the complete collection of words instead of each individual word separately. Try doing a search on *computer virus*. Do not use quotes the first time but use the quotes the second time. You will notice a difference in the number of "hits" (or search results), as well as in the content of each search generated. When searching without quotes, the search engine looks for websites containing any of the words searched for. When quotes are utilized, the search engine limits its search to websites containing all of the words.

Another way to make your search more accurate is to use minus signs. For example, say you want to do a search on tent camping in Michigan. By preceding a word with a minus sign (–), you are specifying that you do *not* want that word as a part of the search. Using this example, the search criteria would look like this: *michigan "tent camping"–detroit*. This search phrase would return the Web pages that include locations in Michigan for tent camping, except for those that mention Detroit.

In addition to using search engines, there are other areas on the Internet that provide resources for research projects. Some sites have a collection of links to a variety of research that is related to its content. For example, the website for the International Society for Technology in Education (ISTE) has teacher planning resources, research on using technology in the classroom, links to similar websites, and more. Online encyclopedias are also an excellent source of information, e.g., Encyclopedia Britannica Online and Wikipedia. Students can also refer to online dictionaries and thesauruses for help with writing.

Searching, not Surfing

It is important to remember that regardless of what you or your students do on the Internet, it needs to have a purpose and to be productive. Teachers must provide clear instructions, precise expectations, and careful supervision. Too often, students are found surfing the Internet with no real direction for what they are trying to accomplish; this is not a worthwhile use of educational time (Dodge, 1997). Be sure to give your students some direction before they begin searching. Instruct them to stay focused on the topic and not become distracted by advertisements, other topics and websites, games, quizzes, chat rooms, or even email. Suggest that they use a search engine and teach them the search strategies outlined above. Another way to add structure to student time on the Internet is to direct your students in a WebQuest. This process is explained later in the chapter under the heading "WebQuests."

Evaluating Results of Searches

It is not enough to know how to use a search engine to find websites. Students also need to learn how to evaluate the results of their searches to see how relevant the websites are to their research questions. "When searching the Internet, we are all miners and engineers. Each of us must know the technique for digging, but also be skilled in seeking out clues so that we can create strategies for knowing where to dig. Perhaps the most important thing to understand about searching for information on the Internet is the fact that it is more like being a detective than being a miner" (Warlick, 2005, p. 110). Teach students how to sort through search results to determine which ones are the best. This teaches them an important practical skill and gives them more practice in critical thinking. Learn the following methods and then teach them to your students.

First of all, look for the keyword(s) or phrase you used to search in each returned result. It will be highlighted in each result. The best results will contain all of the components of your search criteria. Second, most search engines list the search results in the order of relevance. Therefore, focus on the first ten to 15 search results (or hits). Don't waste time with the rest. Start a new search and evaluate the first ten to 15 results of the new search. Third, look at the domain names (i.e., organization names) of the first ten to 15 results. Choose those results that are from the most reliable sources—the following section will provide more information on this. David Warlick (2005) discusses how successful Internet researchers make assumptions about what is available and what clues they will find. They are open to different types and formats of information than they anticipated. They realize the search will be a process with a series of searches, each one revealing new clues.

Evaluating Website Accuracy

While the Internet is a wealth of information, it is not guaranteed to be correct. Therefore, it is very important to make sure that the information that you collect is accurate. The five criteria that you can use to check the accuracy of a website are listed in Table 4.1 (Lamb, 2005).

Table 4.1: Five Criteria for Checking Website Accuracy

Criteria:	Examples:
Accuracy	Can the author be contacted? What is the purpose of this Web page? How accurate is the information? Can the same information be found in other sources?
Authority	Who is the author of the information? Did the author cite his/her sources? Is the author an authority on the information?
Objectivity	How detailed is the information? Are there any biases or opinions stated on the Web page? Is the Web page sponsored or supported by a specific company or organization?
Current	Is there a copyright date on the Web page? When was the Web page last updated? Are all of the links up-to-date?
Coverage	Is the information on the Web page correctly cited and/or referenced? Does the Web page have any advertising? Is the amount of advertising limited? Has the Web page won any awards?

Another way to evaluate a website is to understand the URL (Uniform Resource Locator). Every Web page that is located on the Internet has its own unique address. Each URL or Web address is made up of a series of letters, numbers, words, and forward slashes (/). The URL has three main components: the protocol, the domain name, and the path. The following URL is defined below:

http://www.teachercreatedmaterials.com.

The **protocol** is the first part of the Web address—it consists of the letters "http," which stand for *Hyper Text Transfer Protocol*. It is the format in which the computer transfers Web pages over the Internet. The colon (:) and slashes (//) are separators between the protocol and the domain name.

The **domain name** identifies the computer where the Web page is stored. In the example shown above, the domain name is "teachercreatedmaterials." The "www" at the beginning of the address determines that the hosting computer is set up as a web server. The last part of the domain name is the extension ".com". It signifies what type of organization created or runs the Web page. In this case, the Web page is operated by a business. There are five major domain categories: "edu" = educational institution; "org" = organization or association; "gov" = government; "com" = commercial or business; and "mil" = military. Others include "net" (network), "biz" (business), and "tv" (television).

The **path** is the third part of the Web page address. The above example does not show a path, but here is an example: *http://www.teachercreatedmaterials.com/ technology*. The "technology" part of this address is the path. It determines the exact location of the Web page on the Web server. It follows the extension with a slash (/) and a series of letters, numbers, words, and additional slashes. It will often end with the file extension "html" or "htm," which indicates that the file was created with the coding language that is used to create Web pages. The "html" stands for *Hyper Text Markup Language*.

Why is it important to understand the components of a Web address or URL? Knowing the components of a Web address will help you and your students evaluate if a website or Web page is from a respected organization. For example, let's say you conduct a search on elephants.

If you see a search result from *nationalgeographic.com*, you can be confident that it will have accurate and reliable information. However, the same search will yield other results, some of which will be from organizations you have never heard of or from sites like geocities.com, where Web pages are created by home users, i.e., anybody with access to the Internet.

If you do encounter a URL showing a domain name, i.e., organization name, that you are not familiar with, and it looks like it might have pertinent information, click the link and quickly determine if it's from a respected organization. To do this, scan the website's home page. Often, it will display the organization's name. If it is a museum, governmental body, significant nonprofit organization, significant news organization, or well-respected company, you can probably trust its content. If the organization's name isn't displayed, look at the bottom of the page. The small print will usually state copyright information and the organization that created the page. Another place to look is in the "About Us" section. Some organizations will describe their history, accomplishments, and objectives here.

Finding Missing Web Pages

Knowing how to read a URL can also help you find a missing Web page. If you follow a link or type in a Web address like *http://www.teachercreatedmaterials.com/ technology* and the page no longer exists, try truncating the Web address to search only for the organization. For example, shorten the address to *http://www.teacher createdmaterials.com* by deleting the path "technology." Once you are on the organization's home page, use the organization's search engine to find the page you need. In this case, you would search for "technology." In most cases, the page was moved to a new address and simply starting from the organization's home page will allow you to find it. Knowing the parts of the URL or Web address helps you to change your search slightly and find what you are looking for.

Looking Out for Danger and Fraud

As previously alluded to, websites and chat rooms can be places where fraud and danger lurk. Users face email viruses that can destroy computer hardware, inappropriate websites, computer hackers who are trying to steal identities and personal information, and predators posing as someone else. Teaching students to be critical of information on the Internet will give them the tools they need to protect themselves. A student who is practiced at critiquing websites will develop an automatic radar for danger. However, cautious teacher monitoring will always be necessary, as teachers must protect students from offensive or dangerous material on the Internet and protect their identities (Warlick, 2005). ISTE found that districts vary in their approach to these problems. In some schools, students are only allowed Internet access with adult supervision. Other schools use blocking or filtering software to prevent access to inappropriate websites. Others require students and parents to sign a contract about acceptable Internet use (Moursund & Smith, 2000).

The National Center for Education Statistics (NCES) found that in 2003 almost all public schools with Internet access (97 percent) used various technologies or procedures to control student access to inappropriate material on the Internet (Parsad & Jones, 2005). David Warlick (2005) suggests that teachers go one step further and teach their students the responsibility of not being part of the danger in the future. He mentions that technology-savvy students are often the source of dangerous and costly computer viruses sent through email. "It is our responsibility as educators to teach our children that the information infrastructure is where we live. We depend on it to support our economy, entertainment, friendships, safety, and education. . . . We must teach children to protect the information" (p. 107).

Citing Sources

The first two NETS standards for students under the social, ethical, and human issues category are the following (ISTE, 2000, p. 14):

- Students understand the ethical, cultural, and societal issues related to technology.

- Students practice responsible use of technology systems, information, and software.

As we continue to encourage students to use the Internet as a resource for school projects, we need to remember to reinforce these standards by teaching students the importance of properly citing sources. Tell students that the words, music, and art that they find on the Internet and in other resources are created by people who put a lot of thought and time into their work. By wanting to use other people's work, the students are recognizing that it is something valuable. In order to show their respect for what it is they want to use and for the person who created it, they should always give proper credit.

There are multiple sites on the Internet that help teachers to address these issues with their students. David Warlick's Landmark Project is a website that provides a "Permission Template" that students can use to request permission to use material from a website. To find it online, go to *http://landmark-project.com/permission1.php.*

Be aware that plagiarism is a growing problem. With the ability to cut and paste text, students are quick to highlight, copy, and paste information from an Internet source and place it directly into their own documents. It is also important to teach students that they cannot just copy large sections from an author's work even when citing the source. It is extremely important that students fully understand the concepts of copyright and plagiarism.

Student Projects That Utilize the Internet

This section briefly describes various projects that students can accomplish using the Internet. Included are examples of how the Internet can be a powerful tool for shaping real-world lessons and for developing critical thinking skills.

Participating in Scientific Research

An excellent way to connect your classroom with the real world is to involve students in a genuine ongoing scientific research project found online (Roschelle et al., 2001). As students participate in the project, they will collect data, practice the scientific method, use critical thinking skills, learn important science concepts, develop and apply math skills and concepts, develop respect for scientists and their work, insert themselves into the role of a scientist, and imagine possible future studies or careers.

There are numerous ways to involve students in actual scientific expeditions and research. Students participating in the GLOBE (Global Learning and Observations to Benefit the Environment) program take measurements in their local area, send the data over the Internet, publish research projects, create maps and graphs, and collaborate with scientists around the world (Roschelle et al., 2001). To find out more about GLOBE, simply search the Internet using the keywords "The GLOBE Program."

Other projects that involve students in data gathering include the JASON Project and Global Lab Curriculum. Find more information about these programs by searching using the keywords "The JASON Project" and "Global Lab Curriculum."

The above projects require a significant investment of your time as the teacher. However, there are other less time-consuming ways to involve students in scientific research online. For example, the Center for Innovation in Engineering and Science Education (CIESE) provides several collaborative online research projects for students. At the time of this book's printing, the site offers nine projects spanning different periods of the school year. The projects include: (1) Human Genetics: Students collect data on traits of classmates, compile data from students around the world, and analyze the data to draw conclusions about phenotypes and dominant alleles; and (2) Bucket Buddies: Students collect and test samples of pond water, compile data from students around the world, and draw conclusions to see if the organisms are the same in ponds around the world. To find the CIESE projects, search using the keyword "CIESE" (see Appendix A for direct links to these resources for scientific research).

WebQuests

According to Bernie Dodge (1997), "A WebQuest is an inquiry-oriented activity in which some or all of the information that learners interact with comes from resources on the Internet" (Definitions section). A WebQuest starts with a problem or question and directs students to the online resources needed to answer the question or solve the problem. The emphasis is not on finding information, but instead is intended to challenge students to think about that information in a critical way. "Students usually work in teams, and most WebQuests result in the construction of an information product designed for an authentic audience and to achieve an authentic goal" (Warlick, 2005, p. 221). Bernie Dodge and Tom March developed WebQuests as a way to structure and deepen student learning on the Internet.

According to Dodge (1997), worthwhile WebQuests must have six different components:

1. An introduction to the project

2. An interesting and viable task

3. A set of information sources needed to complete the task, such as websites, experts available via technology, online databases, and even books and other hard-copy materials immediately in the students' vicinity

4. A description of the process students should use to complete the task

5. Information on how to organize the information found

6. A conclusion that invites students to reflect on what they have learned

There are a multitude of WebQuests available on the Internet. They provide an easy way for teachers who are still cautious about using the Internet to get started (Warlick, 2005).

Many WebQuests provide students with outstanding opportunities to learn about and use Internet resources. However, as a classroom teacher, it is very important to evaluate the WebQuest before using it in the classroom. Some questions to ask are:

• Does this WebQuest fit with the goals and objectives of my curriculum?

• What will my students learn from this activity?

- Will the WebQuest activity enhance the learning of my students more than teaching the information to the students in a traditional manner would?

- Will the WebQuest activity cause my students to use higher-order thinking skills and to think critically about the information that they find?

To view sample WebQuests, try doing a search on the phrases "educational webquests" or "teacher webquests." Your hits will include multiple teacher-made WebQuests for all content areas. As you look over the WebQuests, determine if they are comprised of the six different components listed above. Also, see if the problems or questions posed at the beginning of the WebQuest can be answered with the provided resources.

Internet Exchange Projects

Internet Exchange Projects involve collaboration between two or more classrooms that use the Internet to share information. Internet Exchange Projects include Keypals (email pen pals), cross-cultural exchange projects, and any other collaborative project among classes in different schools. Benefits of Internet Exchange Projects are many. By communicating with other classrooms from all over the world, students learn about different cultures and world regions. The students see firsthand how the Internet can bring people together and serve as a valuable source of information. Through the use of email and the sharing of documents, students learn the importance of correct spelling, sentence structure, and topic organization when communicating with others. David Warlick (2005) writes of a fourth-grade classroom in an urban New Jersey school that used email to become "ePals" with students in Italy. That year, the literacy test scores dramatically improved, even above the scores of the previous students of this same teacher. The administration and teachers credited this increase to the use of the email project. "Using a computer with email, and having a peer somewhere in the world is highly motivating to students. They form a new desire and reason to write well—to communicate. Students will learn, when they want to learn, and they will develop skills, when those skills mean something to their lives—right now" (Warlick, p. 68).

There are two ways to initiate an Internet Exchange Project as a class project. You can use an existing Internet Exchange Project website or spontaneously develop a project while communicating with another teacher over the Internet. Website projects are a more permanent form of Internet Exchange Projects. They are regularly available to teachers and their classrooms. Teachers can use them with multiple classes from year to year. The spontaneous projects are not ones already available to teachers. As teachers chat and email over the Internet, they share ideas. As one of these ideas grows into a joint project between the two classrooms, an Internet Exchange Project is spontaneously born.

There are several websites that offer ideas for potential Internet Exchange Projects or participation in existing ones. Some of these sites include Global SchoolNet Internet Projects Registry, the Flat Stanley Project, and the Global Virtual Classroom. Search for one of these online (see Appendix A for specific links).

Below is a detailed project that will hopefully spark additional ideas as to how to integrate Internet Exchange Projects into the classroom.

Student Project: Mystery Regions

This Internet Exchange Project involves collaborating with classrooms from all over the United States or from all over the world. You can start by communicating with other teachers from different regions. While you may know the origin of the different classrooms, the students must discover the mystery regions and determine the actual location of each classroom.

In order to complete this Internet Exchange Project, follow these steps:

- First, connect with multiple teachers from around the country or from around the world. Together, the teachers must decide how the students will communicate and how often. They must also determine how long the project will last. The teachers decide what kinds of questions the students can ask of each other, how the students will answer the questions (complete answers or just *yes* and *no*), and how often they can guess the locations of the mystery classrooms.

- The second step is to have the students generate a list of questions for the mystery classrooms. Depending on the number of classroom computers and mystery classrooms, you will probably need to place the students into teams. Remember that there are many benefits to grouping the students, such as differentiating the lesson for students of different abilities and encouraging group problem solving. Each team is then assigned a specific mystery location.

- The third step is to direct the students to communicate with their individual mystery classrooms. They might ask questions about the local weather, the changing of seasons, natural resources, or local food preferences. As they hear back from their mystery classroom, the students must record the answers. After several questions have been answered, the students can begin to determine the location of the mystery region. At the same time, each group of students will be answering questions via email about their region so that another classroom can figure out where they are located.

- The last step is to have the students use various map resources to help them determine the location of the mystery classroom. If the students think that they have figured out the mystery, they should contact the mystery classroom with their guess. If they are wrong, the students should reevaluate their information to come up with a different location. If the students are correct, then they can continue to communicate with the mystery classroom, asking more specific questions about the particular region.

Hotlists: Direct Students on the Internet

Hotlists are lists of links that help focus students during the learning process. They send students to specific sites that address the same or similar topics. A hotlist directs students to particular teacher-chosen websites that will be used to complete a class activity. Hotlists can also be used to help direct students during a research project. Hotlists save class time—students click on links to navigate to websites rather than type in website addresses. Hotlists are different from WebQuests in that hotlists are lists of resources whereas WebQuests are an entire structured inquiry activity within themselves.

You have a few options when creating a hotlist. One option is to generate a list of URLs on a classroom or district Web page. The hyperlinks will direct the students to specific Web pages so that they can find the answers to a set of questions that the teacher has asked. Another option is to use the website called Filamentality (simply do an online search for "filamentality"). Anyone can access the site in order to create a list of specific sites that provide resources to students and teachers.

To locate existing hotlists on the Internet, try doing a search on the phrases "educational hotlists" or "teacher hotlists." Your hits will include multiple teacher-made, museum-made, or educational organization-made hotlists for many content areas.

Internet Communication Tools

If your students use the Internet, they will most likely be familiar with the tools of communication such as email and instant messaging. However, while students may know how to operate and use these tools, they may not know "netiquette" (i.e., the rules for good emailing behavior), the dangers associated with these tools, how to use them to enhance their education, or the full range of communication power and resources at their fingertips.

Email

Email has become an integral part of communication between teachers, students, parents, and administrators. It allows students to send questions, assignments, papers, and comments to teachers 24 hours a day, seven days a week. Teachers can then reply to the students between classes, in the evenings, or even on weekends. Parents can also have the same type of access to teachers if they have questions or concerns about the progress of their child in school.

Email Dos and Don'ts

Because email is so important to the communication process within a school, it is important to be aware of the dos and don'ts of email, also known as netiquette. There are some starting points listed here. However, a teacher can also type "netiquette" into a search engine to learn more about it, or the class can create an agreement of proper netiquette as a contract. It is important to double-check the accuracy of the email address of the person you are emailing. It can be embarrassing if you send a personal email to the wrong person. Another "do" is to always include a descriptive phrase on the subject line. If a person is short on time and scanning through a list of emails, a descriptive subject line gives the person an idea of the content of the email. It is also common courtesy to reply to all emails within 24 hours, if at all possible.

Another useful tip is to create a separate email address to use exclusively when ordering from the Internet or giving your information to any business or organization. Set up this email account with a free Web-based service like Hotmail, Yahoo!, or Google. When you sign up for something over the Internet, your email address is often sold to other businesses. Your personal email account could then be inundated with junk email. The email account you set up for Internet business will collect all of the unwanted spam, which leaves your personal email account clean.

There are also many "don'ts" when using email. Never send anything in an email that you do not want to be public. People mistakenly believe that email is private and personal. However, no email is private. Even if you delete an email from your computer, an expert can usually find a way to retrieve it.

If you do not recognize the email address of the sender or are not expecting an email with an attachment, even from someone you know, do not open any file that is attached to an email. Viruses lurk in emails and are just waiting to be unleashed onto your computer. They are designed to erase information on your computer or cause your programs to do strange functions.

Also, when writing an email, try not to write words in all capital letters—this is considered to be shouting at the person who is reading the email. Lastly, before sending a very large attachment with an email, it is a good idea to check with the recipient first. That person may be restricted to a specific amount of space on his/her email server.

Discussion Boards

Discussion boards are places on the Internet where computer users can post messages to which others can respond. Users do not have to be online at the same time. There are discussion boards for almost every topic. The topics can range from personal medical matters to intellectual discussions and critiques.

You can use discussion boards to enhance learning by starting a conversation about a topic studied in class. The students are invited (or assigned) to visit the discussion board and add their opinions. This can prepare the students for an upcoming classroom discussion. A related idea is to post a question or problem that is an extension of something studied in class. The students who want to delve a little deeper into the topic can participate in the online discussion. While all students can participate, this is a good way to extend learning for more advanced students. To create a discussion board, try using Nicenet (simply conduct a search for "nicenet"). Many school districts also purchase subscriptions for teachers and students to Blackboard. Blackboard is a fee-based version of Nicenet that allows teachers to create discussion boards and manage entire courses.

As a professional educator, you can access discussion boards to seek advice on lesson plans, classroom management, differentiation, working with colleagues and administrators, and other topics related to your field. To find discussion boards, try searching using the key phrases "teacher discussion board" or "teacher discussion forum."

Teach Students to "Chat" with Caution

Students may decide to participate in discussion boards, chat rooms, or instant messaging outside of school. Advise students to be wary of the people with whom they communicate online. Instruct them to always be aware that people can write anything about themselves—there is no way to verify the identities of people met online. Children and teenagers have been taken advantage of by people pretending to be someone else.

Weblogs

A weblog is also known as a Web log or a blog. It is basically a personal journal Web page. Individuals create Web pages where they can share their personal thoughts or their knowledge on specific topics. "Most frequently, blogs are used as a diary of what people are experiencing, thinking, inventing, feeling, and learning. Most are rants, many are celebrations, and some are serious examinations of issues that you may be teaching, written by experts in the field" (Warlick, 2005, p. 52). Weblogs can be published on Web pages using a free Web server on the Internet, or they can be developed using a blog publishing tool. Once a weblog is created, the owner adds to it at will. The information is usually posted in reverse chronological order.

For teachers and students, weblogs can add an interesting component to online learning. Weblogs can encourage students to publish their writings and share them with peers worldwide. It can create a collaborative online learning environment as multiple students share their own ideas and respond to others. When published by teachers, weblogs can be an open form of communication with students and parents. Teachers can post class-related information like calendars, homework assignments, and project due dates. Teachers can also continue a discussion begun in class. There are blog search engines, such as Bloglines.com that search for topics in blogs. However, teachers should monitor student use as every topic is freely discussed (Warlick, 2005).

Listservs

Listservs are similar to weblogs—individuals post ideas and questions and others read the postings and respond. However, unlike weblogs, listservs are not run from Web pages. Listserv messages are sent and received through email programs. Therefore, in order to receive emails from a listserv, you have to sign up. Your name will then be put on an electronic mailing list.

To become part of a listserv, you must send an email message requesting a subscription to the list. After your subscription has been accepted, the person who monitors the list will send you a "welcome letter" that explains how that particular listserv works. All email messages sent to the list will be distributed to all subscribers' email inboxes. You are able to unsubscribe from the listserv at any time. If you sign up for multiple listservs or any that send a large number of messages, you may want to maintain a separate email account dedicated to your listserv accounts.

Chat Rooms

A chat room is a place on the Internet where you can have live conversations with multiple people at the same time. It is like having a conference call, except that you are typing on a keyboard rather than talking into a phone. Everyone who is in the chat room can see what you type.

Chat rooms are one of the most interactive areas on the Internet, and a favorite location for teachers and students to interact with their peers. There are different levels of supervision in chat rooms—some are open environments with no moderation, others have leaders who moderate the discussion, and still others have monitors who assess what people write before anyone else sees it. If individuals in the chat room misbehave, the monitors can warn them or bar them from further participation.

For teachers, a chat room is an excellent place to share ideas with colleagues. It is also a place where teachers can interact with their students and help them with homework questions. For students, a chat room can become an interactive classroom. They can meet up with an expert and discuss various topics that they are learning in school.

There are, however, concerns about using chat rooms. Students and the chat rooms that they use must be monitored. It is important for teachers to choose chat rooms that are student-friendly. Students should be warned not to give out personal information, as the others involved may not be who they claim to be. Student-friendly chat rooms have a strong monitoring system built in to the environment. This helps to prevent the use of inappropriate language and topics within the chat room.

Instant Messaging

Instant messaging is software that lets a person instantly send messages from one computer to another. It is a form of instant email where one talks with someone in real time, and it is very popular with both children and adults. When you log on to your computer, the instant messaging program lets you know when your friends or family are online, usually by playing a specific sound. A small window will appear which allows you to send them short messages.

There are many ways to use the Internet in your class-room to broaden and deepen student learning. However, as you have read, the Internet is a powerful tool, and like all powerful tools, there are certain ways to use it efficiently and effectively. From guiding student research to making use of tools like discussion boards, you can harness the power of the Internet for your classroom. Finally, remember that it takes time. Teachers are often surprised at how much student learning time is required before students begin to make effective use of the Internet to learn other subject areas (Moursund & Smith, 2000).

Chapter Four Reflection

1. How could you use email to increase understanding and share ideas?

   _____

   _____

   _____

2. How would incorporating hotlists, Internet Exchange Projects, and WebQuests into your teaching benefit you and your students?

   _____

   _____

   _____

3. In what ways will integrating the Internet into your classroom activities help to improve students' problem-solving and critical thinking skills?

   _____

   _____

   _____

4. Explain how using the Internet and communicating through technology can help to improve your productivity and that of your students.

   _____

   _____

   _____

Assessing Project-Based Learning

The term assessment means to effectively measure student learning using a variety of tools, such as academic standards, rubrics, teacher observations, performance assessments, portfolios, and traditional tests. Effective teachers use the data from student assessments and reflection of their own teaching to plan and conduct their further teaching objectives (Norman & Hayden, 2002). Assessment tends to make teachers groan as they consider high-stakes state standardized testing and the increasing pressure to perform well. Many districts are pushing the teachers of students who are low-performing to move to scripted content programs with little room for teaching creativity. The public criticizes teachers who spend all year teaching to the test but also hold the test results in esteem. However, there is also a growing movement to shift away from spending the entire school year in preparation for the multiple-choice testing and rather toward promoting higher-order thinking skills in the classroom. These critical skills prepare students for real-life problem solving. Educational reformers summon teachers to align curriculum content, instructional methods, and assessment. Recently, this move for change has shaped the foundation for a growing emphasis on *authentic assessment*. Authentic assessments are defined as performance-based, realistic, and instructionally appropriate (Moursund & Smith, 2000). Students have a wider range of ability than they can show on a standardized assessment. "In order to show these capabilities, however, they need learning environments which are responsive to the many individual differences which influence learning" (Chard & Katz, 2001, Learning section, para. 2). Project-based learning using technology is one compelling way to approach authentic skills being assessed in genuine ways.

How is project-based learning involving technology best assessed? This chapter offers answers to that question. In addition, this chapter explores how technology can be an assessment tool and touches on how to use technology for testing and for helping students create ePortfolios.

Check Your Knowledge

Directions: Evaluate the accuracy of each statement below. Place a T (for True) or an F (for False) in the space provided.

_____ 1. Assessment rubrics only benefit the teacher, not the students.

_____ 2. Before creating a rubric, it is important for the teacher to know which performance criteria he/she wants to evaluate.

_____ 3. The ISTE NETS for Students performance indicators can provide a teacher with performance criteria when developing a rubric for a lesson involving technology.

_____ 4. When students are given a rubric before they start a project, they have a better understanding of the teacher's expectations.

_____ 5. Objective tests can effectively measure critical thinking skills.

_____ 6. Online testing results can be more beneficial to skilled computer users.

_____ 7. Receiving an immediate report of students' test scores is an advantage to an online testing program.

_____ 8. Electronic portfolios (or ePortfolios) are not assessments in themselves, but a collection of work to be assessed.

_____ 9. Work that the students have done collaboratively can be duplicated and saved in multiple students' ePortfolios.

_____ 10. Eportfolios usually become very large files because of the different images that are included.

Project-Based Learning and Assessments

Project-based learning is powerful. Sylvia Chard and Lilian Katz (2001) define a project as "an in-depth investigation of a real-world topic worthy of children's attention and effort" (Definition section, para. 1). Students who are engaged in project-based learning take on challenging, interesting tasks. They use the appropriate tools, often technological ones. During the project, they engage in discussing, analyzing, problem solving, and drawing conclusions in groups and individually. This type of learning prepares them to problem solve, construct meaning, and communicate with others now and in the future. There is growing agreement that problem solving and other higher-order skills should be given more importance (Moursund & Smith, 2000). Project-based learning takes time. Some of the most important learning that happens may not automatically be demonstrated on state standardized testing. "This does not reflect poorly on project-based learning, it reflects poorly on the prevailing nature of educational assessment. But that's another issue" (Warlick, 2005, p. 216).

This vision of project-based learning using technology is a constant theme throughout this book, but an important piece of project-based learning has been missing thus far—assessment. "Projects, like good stories, have a beginning, a middle, and an end. This temporal structure helps the teacher to organize the progression of activities according to the development of the children's interests and personal involvement with the topic of study" (Chard & Katz, 2001, Three Phases section, para. 1). The "end" is the assessment. Without the assessment piece, student projects will have little focus, students will have little direction, and the results will be below par.

However, before diving into how to assess project-based learning, let's review different types of assessments.

Different Types of Assessments

Traditional forms of assessment are usually what we think of when we discuss measuring student learning. Traditional testing includes objective tests, which contain questions for which there is only one correct answer (e.g., multiple choice, true and false, fill-in-the-blank, and short-answer questions). This type of testing measures student knowledge of a particular topic. These tests are often summative, meaning they only test the end result of the learning process. While objective testing does have its place at times, it cannot effectively measure the wide range of skills that students should be learning in school. It certainly cannot measure critical thinking, problem-solving, or communication skills effectively.

Another form of assessment is subjective tests. Subjective testing relies on the teacher's judgment for assessing the students' knowledge. The questions are usually short-answer or essay questions and tend to be more open-ended. This type of testing can help measure student thought processes and critical thinking skills. However, it offers one view of what a student has learned and is limited to what a student can clearly express in writing.

Yet another form of assessment is authentic or performance-based assessment. This is how project-based learning is best assessed. An authentic assessment can measure student effort, problem-solving skills, speaking skills, comprehension of the learning objectives, and the student's ability to draw conclusions and create solutions. These assessments also lend themselves to being formative, meaning that they assess student progress throughout the learning process. The process of using authentic assessments can include rubrics, portfolios, and ePortfolios.

Project-Based Learning Assessments: Rubrics, Portfolios, and Eportfolios

The tools and methods for assessing project-based learning are explained in the following paragraphs. Above all, assessments should be based on students' performance of real tasks. The entire course of the project should be assessed, not just the end product (McKenzie, 1998). The following components of assessing project-based learning help accomplish these important goals.

Rubrics

The assessment component of a project or other authentic learning experience guides the entire learning process. Usually the guidelines for a project are spelled out in a rubric. "In short it is a list of objectives, what the student will learn or learn to do as a result of completing the assignment. For each objective, a rubric will also list performance indicators, observable evidence that the student has gained the objective knowledge and/or skills to varying degrees, each degree having an assigned number of points leading to a grade" (Warlick, 2005, p. 236). Assessment rubrics list the appropriate performance criteria for student success. Rubrics provide objective guidelines to measure and evaluate student understanding. They also improve learning because students have an opportunity to see the project expectations before the project is due (Stiggins, 1997). The students can review the guidelines as they complete their work. "Authentic assignments also lend themselves especially well to the use of student-produced rubrics and the resulting authentic assessments. The student's goals can become part of the rubric's goals, with teacher- or student-defined benchmarks. This gives students a ruler with which to measure their success and teachers have a tool to assess the students' learning" (Warlick, 2005, p. 162).

Teachers who consistently use rubrics believe that they improve students' end products and therefore increase learning (Goodrich, 1997). When teachers use rubrics to evaluate papers or projects, they know specifically what makes an acceptable final product and why. By giving the students the rubric before they start their projects, they are being given the opportunity to know how they will be evaluated and can prepare accordingly. The students can better match their efforts to teacher expectations if standards and rubrics are clearly explained from the beginning (McKenzie, 1998). Developing a grid and making it available as a tool for student use will provide the scaffolding necessary to improve the quality of their work and increase their knowledge. Rubrics can prove to be useful tools as teachers lead students to complete projects involving technology. Rubrics can measure the knowledge and critical thinking skills that teachers hope the students will develop while working on the assigned project or problem. Keep in mind that rubrics can also measure the technology skills and knowledge that teachers are responsible for teaching.

How to Create a Rubric

Before creating a rubric, you will need to determine the performance criteria. Generate a list of items of what you expect the students to do as they work on the project. Then generate another list of items of what you expect the final project to have or look like. Once you have these two lists, highlight items of major importance and eliminate items of minimal importance. The final number of performance criteria is up to you. However, the more detailed the list, the more involved the scoring process.

Figure 5.1 on page 128 shows a sample rubric for the Disneyland in Space project described in Chapter 3. Note that this rubric also provides space for student self-assessment as well as peer assessment.

Figure 5.1: Sample "Disneyland in Space" Rubric and Scoring Sheet

Disneyland in Space Rubric and Scoring Sheet

Criteria	Small Fry 0–4 Points	Medium Fry 5–7 Points	Big Fry 8–10 Points	Self Score	Peer Score	Teacher Score
Gave the distance from Earth to each planet.	Gave the distance for one planet.	Gave the distance for two planets.	Gave the distance for three planets.			
Described the surface features and temperature of each planet.	Described the surface features and temperatures of one planet.	Described the surface features and temperature of two planets.	Described the surface features and temperatures of three planets.			
Discussed the availability of water for each planet.	Discussed the availability of water on one planet.	Discussed the availability of water on two planets.	Discussed the availability of water on three planets.			
Described each planet's climate.	Described the climate of one planet.	Described the climate of two planets.	Described the climate of three planets.			
Described interesting places on each planet.	Described interesting places on one planet.	Described interesting places on two planets.	Described interesting places on all three planets.			
Stated the planet chosen for Disneyland and stated why.	Did not attempt to answer this question.	Selected a planet but did not explain why.	Selected a planet and explained why.			
Presentation Text	Text was difficult to read.	Text was easy to read but did not enhance presentation.	Text was easy to read, and it enhanced the presentation.			
Presentation Graphics	Did not have graphics.	Contained some graphics, but they did not enhance presentation.	Contained graphics that enhanced the presentation.			
Presentation Sounds	No sounds were used.	Sounds were not relevant or easy to understand.	Sounds were relevant, clear, and easy to understand.			
Presentation Transitions	No transitions were used.	Transitions were not relevant.	Transitions were very relevant.			
Comment Box			TOTAL SCORE			

Excerpted from *TechTools: Resource Kit for Microsoft PowerPoint*. Copyright © 2003 by Teacher Created Materials, Inc.

When creating a rubric, many teachers prefer to use four-point or five-point scales. Rubrics that list fewer performance levels are often too restrictive. They do not easily accommodate students with varying learning abilities. Rubrics that list more than five performance levels tend to be too detailed, which makes them more difficult to create and use when evaluating. They would also be difficult when students are using them for self-evaluation. Be sure each performance level is well-defined. Start with the lowest performance level. Determine exactly what you will not accept as a completed project. Next, create the performance-level criteria for the second-highest or third-highest level. At this point, determine exactly what average performance criteria you can expect from all of the students. This level defines the acceptable final project. The next step is to create the performance-level criteria for the highest point on the scale. You should determine exactly what makes an outstanding or "above and beyond" project. Then, create the performance-level criteria for other categories within the point scale. Finally, evaluate the performance criteria on either side (high or low) of the point scale to fill in any level you feel is incomplete. Determine if you need to create a performance level between any two existing ones.

It is important to realize that a rubric is always a work-in-progress. Each time it is used, reevaluate it and modify it to fit your revised expectations of the students and their projects. Once your rubric is completed, be sure to share it with students before they start their project. Expectations must be clear from the beginning of the project. The students should be able to compare their progress to a model (McKenzie, 1998).

Technology software can be a great asset for teachers designing rubrics. You can create rubrics using word processing, desktop publishing, or spreadsheet software. Word processing programs allow you to make tables to display the various levels of the performance criteria. If you are using a spreadsheet, simply create a grid with the appropriate number of rows and columns (depending on the number of performance criteria you have created), then fill in the boxes. See Appendix B for online rubric resources to help you get started on creating your own rubrics.

Technology Performance Criteria

Of course, the ISTE NETS for students is an excellent place to turn when looking for technology-related performance criteria for your rubrics. Remember that the technology skills the students will use during the project are just one piece of what you are assessing. Your rubric should also contain curriculum-based learning objectives and perhaps critical thinking skills, communication skills, and student effort. If the project is large, consider creating different rubrics to assess different areas of learning. Especially useful to you will be the ISTE performance indicators, which are outlined in the student profiles (see Chapter Two for a listing of various examples of performance indicators students should master through different grade levels). Refer also to the ISTE website for the student profiles and performance indicators of all the grade levels. Find the performance indicators that correlate to your lesson and then rewrite them in more specific terms to create your performance criteria.

You can view a rubric of technology skills and knowledge that is based on the NETS for students. The rubric correlates each of the ISTE NETS for students with the appropriate skills that the PreK–12 students should be able to accomplish. Search online using the key phrase "NETS for Students: Achievement Rubric."

Portfolios and Eportfolios

In recent years, there has been an emphasis on using portfolios and ePortfolios (or electronic portfolios) to assess students engaged in authentic or project-based learning. Portfolios are collections of student work and the products of their learning. Typically, the students select the pieces that they feel best represent their learning and skill. Portfolio pieces are usually best assessed using rubrics.

Eportfolios are digital portfolios that are stored on computers. They can contain presentations, writings, and other products that students have constructed using the computer. They can also contain artwork or other products that have been scanned and stored digitally.

It is important to note that the products that the students create on the computer can be used in either a hard copy portfolio or an ePortfolio. The students do not have to create ePortfolios to collect and store the products they make with a computer. If the students are not creating ePortfolios, instruct them to print the products they feel best represent their learning and store the hard copies in their portfolios.

More About Eportfolios

There are three distinct advantages to having students create ePortfolios: ease of storage, use of multimedia skills, and use of computer skills. With a traditional portfolio, a student collects items that showcase his/ her talents and then puts them in a large folder, binder, or box. Eportfolios allow the information to be stored digitally on a floppy disk, zip disk, CD, or portable drive (e.g., a jump or flash drive). Eportfolios not only take up little physical space, but they also hold a great deal of information. Pictures, artwork, and writing samples can be scanned, saved, and later imported into the software program. Eportfolios can be transferred to future teachers in years ahead to show growth through grade levels. Samples of students reading orally can be recorded and saved to the ePortfolio as audio files. Another important component of an ePortfolio is that work that students have done collaboratively can be duplicated and placed into each of the students' portfolios.

In order to create an ePortfolio, the teacher and the students will need access to different types of hardware and software. When checking for the correct hardware components, the teacher's computer should have as much memory (RAM) as possible. This allows the computer to run the necessary software and external devices without freezing up. Since ePortfolios tend to be large in size, the computer should also have a large hard drive, a CD burner, or at least one USB port to attach a jump drive so that all of the students' files can be saved in one location. If a student plans to add video to his/her ePortfolio, it is also important that the computer have video input and output ports. A flatbed scanner is also a very valuable hardware device. The student or teacher can use the scanner to turn paper assignments and photos into digital images. A digital camera can be used to take still pictures or to capture video that can be added to the student's ePortfolio.

Consider having the students create an ePortfolio (or traditional portfolio) to showcase any type of computer product. You might have them include multimedia products from programs such as PowerPoint, HyperStudio, Kid Pix, DreamWeaver, or FrontPage. You can also encourage them to include products made with word processors (e.g., Microsoft Word and AppleWorks), graphic organizer software (e.g., Inspiration and Kidspiration), and movie creators (e.g., iMovie and Director).

The next step in the process of creating an ePortfolio is planning. In other words, this is not a task that you should start in the last two months of the school year! There are several things to consider. The students and teacher need to determine exactly which items will be included in the ePortfolio. It is important to include pictures of the individual students, pictures or videos of the students' projects, and electronic or scanned versions of the students' papers and assignments. The students also need to create a storyboard to help determine the order of their slides, cards, or pages, depending on what type of software they are using.

Before the students begin to create their ePortfolios, make sure that the computers and software are working and ready for the students. While this project is extremely rewarding, it can easily become a nightmare if the technology is not ready when the students are.

As assignments and projects are completed, graded, and returned to the students, convert them to the digital format. This eliminates the need to do all of the documents for all of the students at one time at the end of the school year. Also, decide how the digital documents and files will be stored until they are placed in the ePortfolio. Because the digital files can be quite large, investigate using the school network, a specified hard drive location, or jump drives to store the students' files.

The last step for the teacher is to decide how the ePortfolio will be evaluated. A rubric is recommended. While the students will have varying levels of academic and technological skills, the assessment component should be equal for all students. The rubric should be given to the students at the onset of the ePortfolio assignment, so they will have a complete understanding of the teacher's expectations.

Once you have organized the students' work, the ePortfolio can be assembled. With the help of multimedia software, the ePortfolio can be enhanced by adding sound, music, pictures, graphics, and even video. The compilation of all of these elements helps to make it more interesting and visually appealing to the student, parent, and teacher.

Electronic portfolios also serve to enhance computer and technology skills. The teacher and students gain the experience of using a variety of hardware and software products by creating, selecting, organizing, editing, and evaluating the portfolios. The students begin to feel a sense of accomplishment by sharing and presenting their ePortfolios to their teacher, classmates, and parents.

Technological Tools That Can Be Used to Assess Students

Technology has multiple functions in assessment. Students can create products using technology that you can then assess using a portfolio and/or rubric. But, there are also technological tools that can help you assess your students. Ideas for using these in the classroom are described below.

Concept Maps

Try using concept maps created with a graphic organizer software program (e.g., Inspiration) to assess student learning. Direct the students to create a concept map showing their prior knowledge of a topic before beginning instruction on that topic. Then, after the lesson or unit, instruct the students to create a concept map again showing their new understanding of the same topic. The result will be a clear view of how much they have learned and how well integrated their understanding has become (Thornburg, 2002).

Online Testing

There are several companies that offer online testing services. While some programs utilize random test question generators (for example, in math programs), others use a bank of possible test questions for teachers to choose from that can be distinguished by content area, instructional level, instructional objective, difficulty of item, and more (Moursund & Smith, 2000).

Using computers to administer tests has several distinct advantages. You can alter the test questions or content to meet the needs of all students. You and your students can receive an immediate reporting of the test scores. Some computer-adaptive testing has the ability to adjust to the performance level of the test taker, quickly choosing questions that are appropriate to the level of knowledge of the test taker (Moursund & Smith, 2000). You can elect to electronically transfer test results to your email or grade book program. The quick turnaround of online test results will help you adapt teaching methods and curricula to meet the needs of individual students.

There are disadvantages to online testing as well. A primary disadvantage can be the cost involved in the start-up and maintenance of the hardware and the software. Also, there is a chance that stored assessment data can be lost if the computer system crashes. In addition, computer access could become an issue. Students who have more experience with computers tend to be better keyboarders and might have an advantage with computer-based tests over those who lack access and skills. As with all tools at the disposal of the teacher, it is best to use online testing along with other methods for evaluating students.

Interactive Response Systems

Quite often, classroom assessments consist of paper-and-pencil tests. However, with the use of an Interactive Response System (IRS), the traditional paper-and-pencil test does not have to be the only form of objective-based assessments. The IRS consists of a receiver unit and a classroom set of response pads. You can ask the students a series of questions, project the questions onto a television or video screen, or provide the students with a paper version of the test. To answer the questions, the students point their response pads toward the receiver unit and press the button that corresponds with their answers. The receiver logs the students' answers on the teacher's computer and then tallies each student's correct and incorrect answers.

By using the Interactive Response System in the classroom, the teacher breaks up the monotony of classroom lectures. The teacher also gets an instant tally of correct and incorrect answers. This provides a way for teachers to check for understanding and adjust the content delivery through the lesson. Struggling readers have the advantage of hearing the question and displaying their content knowledge. It also allows the students to provide anonymous responses to the teacher's questions. This helps to encourage complete classroom participation. The information can be used to determine if a certain concept or objective should be retaught.

Student Self-Assessment

With a tool as powerful as technology, the teacher should not be the only one assessing progress. This book has continually referred to technology as a way to build higher-level thinking and critical thinking skills. Therefore, students need to be using these skills to monitor their own progress on specific projects as well as their overall technology use. The students should have some responsibility in assessing progress and quality. This may be the most difficult component for a teacher to include in a learning-based project, but it is highly worth the effort (Warlick, 2005). Student assessment can take the form of self-evaluation and/or peer evaluation. Students need to learn how to shape and improve their own efforts (McKenzie, 1998). David Warlick mentions an Internet Project contest, called the International Schools Cyberfair sponsored by Global SchoolNet, where the participants also act as the judges. When a class registers to participate, they receive other entries to judge according to a rubric. They are charged with the task of evaluating the others as seriously as they hope to be evaluated. "Many teachers have reported that the evaluation process was just as valuable to their students as building their community web site" (Warlick, p. 39).

As you can see, there are many ways to use technology to assess students. Assessment should be ongoing and frequent. Vigilant teachers monitor throughout the project, changing teaching strategies and asking students to adjust their efforts. Teachers should employ assessment as a tool to further support development in the project (McKenzie, 1998). Educational reformers have emphasized the need for alternatives to multiple-choice questions. Some of these alternatives include student self-evaluation, open-ended questions, student writing projects, explanation of the reasoning behind their problem-solving work, use of rubrics, and portfolio assessment (Moursund & Smith, 2000). Add these tools to your repertoire to obtain a clearer picture of student progress.

Chapter Five Reflection

1. What are some advantages to using an ePortfolio as a student assessment?

   _____

   _____

   _____

2. What do you think is the most important step in creating a rubric? Explain why you think so.

   _____

   _____

   _____

3. Briefly compare objective assessments, subjective assessments, and project-based assessments.

   _____

   _____

   _____

4. How would you assess the effectiveness of online testing programs?

   _____

   _____

   _____

Manage Your Classroom Using Technology

Remember that a computer, or any form of technology, is a learning tool and not a teacher. Computers enhance the learning environment, they do not directly teach. Computers can assist you to better present or share information with your students.

Along this same vein, a computer by itself cannot manage your classroom nor do your paperwork. However, computers can certainly assist you with these professional duties. In fact, a single computer can significantly reduce your workload and help keep you and your students organized. Keep in mind that there are also other forms of technology that can help you. Read this chapter to learn ways in which a computer and other forms of technology can help you manage your classroom, manage your students, and complete administrative tasks. Also included in this chapter are tips for where to place computers in your classroom and how to schedule student access to computers.

Check Your Knowledge

Directions: Evaluate the accuracy of each statement below. Place a T (for True) or an F (for False) in the space provided.

_____ 1. The term *technology* refers only to computers.

_____ 2. You must be completely computer literate before trying to use one to accomplish organizational and administrative tasks.

_____ 3. Even with just one computer in the classroom, many useful duties can be accomplished.

_____ 4. Technology gadgets can also help you manage your classroom.

_____ 5. Student access to a computer should be equal for all students.

_____ 6. One online teacher tool can randomly select which student will give an answer during a classroom discussion.

_____ 7. Well-defined project tasks with scheduled computer time are better than large, ill-defined projects with unscheduled computer time.

_____ 8. It is difficult to do cooperative learning activities using computers.

_____ 9. Test and activity sheet generators, either online or as software, can save a teacher a large amount of time.

_____ 10. Creating bookmarks, or favorites, prevents the students from wasting time when accessing the Internet during class activities.

Use Technology to Manage Your Classroom

Technology can be an integral tool for classroom management. By using technology and a variety of software programs, you can simplify the process of getting your classroom ready before the school year starts. In one study, teachers were surveyed and indicated that they recognized the importance of computer technology in teacher-related functions such as attendance-taking and record-keeping, communication, research and planning, and classroom instruction (Ascione, 2005).

The research shows countless ways that technology can be of use to teachers in preparation for teaching in the classroom. If you are not comfortable using a computer, select one or two simple tasks to try first and do the rest in the traditional manner. As the school year progresses, try to use the computer to complete a few more tasks. After a while, you will be able to use the computer to help you with many organizational and administrative tasks, and you will save yourself a great deal of time and energy.

Getting Ready Before School Starts

As a teacher, you think about your classroom and your students weeks before the doors open for the first day of school. You are anxious to get your classroom ready and organized. By turning to technology, your preparation time can be significantly reduced.

For example, try using word processing or spreadsheet software to create seating charts, class lists, and class schedules. At the elementary level, use a word processor to generate desk name tags, student name tags, "Welcome" signs, and an initial letter for parents. Use preprinted sticker name tags to quickly label any supplies that the students bring into the classroom on the first day or later. A spreadsheet can be used easily to create a scheduling chart during parent conference week. It can also be used to create a chart for classroom library checkout. Use desktop publishing to create visual displays of content standards and lesson objectives that you will be addressing throughout the year.

At the middle school and high school levels, you can begin preparing multimedia presentations to communicate class rules, teacher expectations, or an overview of the semester or school year. You can also set up electronic grade books using rosters of students' names. Use this time to prepare some of the learning tools your students will frequently use during the year. For example, an English teacher can use word processing or multimedia programs for creating organizers that can facilitate the writing process. Both programs have advanced chart and graphic display functions (Brabec, Fisher, & Pitler, 2004). Create rubrics, reflection papers, checklists, or other tools that students will use for self-assessment or recurring classroom processes. Chapter Five discussed extensively the use of rubrics. Teachers can use various software programs to create rubrics. Rubrics can also be created for cooperative groups to assess their own effectiveness at working in a team (Brabec et al.). For lesson planning, look up websites of textbook publishers. These often have suggested activities, organized by chapter and unit. "Suggested activities can provide cues for students to activate prior knowledge and anticipate new content; unit and chapter outlines available on these sites also can serve as advance organizers" (Brabec et al., p. 9).

Further Ways to Use Technology in Your Classroom

With all of the responsibilities that teachers have, a computer can be a major asset to classroom management. By using technology, you can accomplish almost every task that you are expected to do. Tables 6.1 and 6.2 display only some of the ways in which technology can help teachers. Table 6.1 focuses on technology specific to your computer, while Table 6.2 focuses on online (Internet) applications.

Table 6.1: Ways to Use Technology in the Classroom

Application	Activity or Product
Word Processor	Nameplates for students' desks Introduction letters for the students and parents Classroom rules Daily schedule Lesson plans Tests and activity sheets Class reports Communication with parents Labels Classroom newsletters
Spreadsheets	Student task charts Seating charts Lesson plans Grade book Graphs and charts Checklists Flash cards Bingo cards Collection of student data
Multimedia Presentations	Presentations of course content Topic review—game show quiz presentations Printed lecture handouts Tutorials, reviews, or quizzes Open house presentation for parents Student presentations and reports
Databases	Student contact information Business cards Flash cards Lesson plans Classroom inventory Classroom library catalog
Other Software	Electronic grade book programs Graphic organizers (Inspiration/Kidspiration) Testing programs

The Internet also provides an unlimited number of class-room management tools. By doing an Internet search, it is very easy to locate online applications that can help you manage your daily classroom activities.

Table 6.2: Online Applications for the Classroom

Online Applications	Purpose
Rubric Generators	Help teachers define and categorize the specific expectations for a project so that there is a standard evaluation for all students.
Activity Sheet and Test Generators	Help teachers create activity sheets and tests from a preexisting database of questions or concepts from which the teacher chooses.
Classroom Timers	Project an electronic timer onto the computer screen.
Random Number Generators	Generate and display a random number on the computer screen.
Random Student Selectors	Generate and display a random student name on the computer screen.
Class Notes	Allow teachers to post class notes and assignments on the Internet.
Survey Generators	Store teacher- or student-made surveys and tally the responses.
Grade Books	Allow students, parents, and teachers to access grades and classroom information over the Internet.

Technology Peripherals

In addition to computers, there are many other forms of technology that can assist with classroom management. Here we focus on *peripherals*. Peripherals are devices you can use with a computer, such as digital cameras. Several are listed in Table 6.3. Although there is often a wide price range depending on available components, most can be purchased for under $300.

The development of digital technology has expanded the use of video, photography and simulations supporting active learning environments. These emerging technologies address multiple learning styles and active participation leading to knowledge construction and increased understanding. . . . Other technologies such as videoconferencing and virtual environments are leading to new thinking about how students can connect to experts, peers, and teachers. (Norman & Hayden, 2002, p. 323)

Even Physical Education teachers can join the technology fun. "Health and physical education teachers can use instruments such as pedometers and heart rate monitors to collect data on student activity levels to generate and test hypotheses about exercise and health" (Brabec et al., 2004, p. 10).

Table 6.3: Technology Peripherals

Gadget	Purpose
Digital Camera	The teacher can take pictures of new students on first day of school and post student pictures and names on a bulletin board in the classroom.
	The teacher and the students can take pictures of classroom activities and student projects.
	The teacher can take pictures of various steps in an activity to guide student progress.
Flash Drive or Jump Drive	The teacher can use this portable data storage device to store student files and projects.
Label Maker	The teacher can label students' supplies and other classroom items.
Video Converter or Data Projector	This device can be used to transmit the computer image onto a television screen or large screen.
Copier, Scanner, Printer	These can make copies of student papers when the teacher needs extras.
	They can scan photos or student work for student portfolios.
	They can print computer documents.
Electronic Keyboard	The students can use this to type their journals, essays, or assignments without having to sit at a computer (e.g., DreamWriter or AlphaSmart).
CD Burner	This can store school data files on a CD at the end of the school year. It can also be used to create student portfolios.
Computer Microscope	This can transmit images under the microscope onto a computer monitor or television.
Document Camera	This camera projects images of paper, books, photographs, or other objects onto the screen. It does not need to use transparencies, like an overhead. You can even use a pointer or finger to point on the image.
	The teacher can model the writing process and edit students' papers in whole-class lessons (e.g., Elmo).
Electronic Whiteboard	This device allows the teacher to display what is on the computer screen, but also allows the teacher to control the computer from the electronic whiteboard.
	It encourages more interaction with the material on the screen. The teachers and the students can highlight or underline information (e.g. Smart Boards are commercial versions of electronic whiteboards and are increasingly used in education.).

The Use of Email and Online Aids for Teacher Professional Activities

Email is fast becoming a vital part of communication. It can be an integral system of communication for teachers. Teachers, who spend most of their workday apart from other adults, can use email to keep in touch with colleagues, exchanging ideas and asking for support. Schoolwide or district information can be quickly spread through email updates. "In addition, teachers should be able to communicate via email with individual pupils, a group of pupils, the entire class, and with parents (both individually and collectively)" (Zimmerman & Goodman, 2001, para. 7). It might be a good idea to set up a free individual email account to use expressly for the purpose of student and parent contact. This will keep your personal email account free of work-related matters. "One of the problems in parent-teacher communication is the unavailability of the teacher during most of the school day. With email, the parent can leave a message and the teacher can respond when not directly working with pupils or on other professional tasks" (Zimmerman & Goodman, para. 12).

Sometimes schools have their own websites for parents and students to access. School websites often have content standards and district resources. Teachers can create classroom websites as well. There are various companies that will host school and individual teacher Web pages for a fee. Homework policies and daily assignments can be posted by classroom (Brabec et al., 2004). The teacher can keep parents informed about content, and students can check the websites for homework updates, links to additional websites related to the specific units of study, and study tips.

Helpful Tips for Using Computers in the Classroom

Classroom Layout of Computers

In most schools, a teacher may have one to five computers in the classroom. The computers are often placed in a corner or against a back wall. If at all possible, computers have a better impact if they are placed systematically around the room.

Placing computers around the classroom provides students the opportunity to access them without interrupting instruction. It also gives students enough space at each computer so that they can work in groups of two or three and not be overcrowded. Another placement option is to organize the computers into center-type areas. The centers allow the students to work on different activities around the room without distracting others.

The placement of computers in the classroom should also benefit the teacher. It is very important to have one computer close to the teacher's desk. This gives the teacher the opportunity to use it during the day for teaching and classroom management. If possible, it is helpful to have the computers on moveable carts so that they can be moved around the room easily. Also, it is a good idea to make sure that the teacher can see the computer screens from several different directions. This helps to keep the students on task, because the teacher can easily monitor what they are doing on the computer (Tousignant, 1996). Remember to always check with district or school technology specialists before moving computers. Sometimes outlets and wall jacks require the computers to remain in one place.

Scheduling Computer Time

Computer equity is very important in the educational environment. Whether the teacher has one or multiple computers in the classroom, all of the students should have equal access to the computers.

There are several ways to manage computer access in the classroom. One suggestion is to make sure that students have already determined what they are going to do before they get on the computer. Nothing wastes valuable computer time more than sitting at the computer unprepared to work on the assigned project. If the teacher creates bookmarks of project-related Internet links or posts links as favorites, this can prevent students from wasting time when accessing the Internet during class activities. Rather than searching endlessly for sites related to the content, the student can spend valuable computer time actually researching the content. Another option is to limit student access to the computers to 15 to 20 minutes each day, unless they are working on a large project. Put a timer next to each computer. As students sit down to use the computers, set the timer so that it notifies them when their time is up. Another alternative is to have a rotating schedule during the week. Create a timetable that gives each student five different specified times on the computer during the week (Tousignant, 1996). Keep a visible schedule so that students can plan ahead for their specified time. Have them log in and report what they plan to do. Then they can log out and write down what they actually accomplished.

Above all, the best way to ensure that students utilize precious computer scheduled time is to create specific expectations and project directions. Well-defined project tasks with scheduled computer time are better than large, ill-defined projects with unscheduled computer time.

One-Computer Classroom

While many educators would like to have multiple computers in their classrooms, there are times when they only have access to one. It is important to recognize that one computer is better than no computer at all. There are plenty of activities that you can do with only one computer in the classroom.

A single computer is a significant help to you for classroom management and administrative tasks. You can use the computer to record grades and to print student progress reports. A single computer will help you communicate with parents through letters, newsletters, or email. Through the use of software programs or the Internet, you can create lesson plans and generate activity sheets, puzzles, rubrics, and tests.

A single classroom computer can also assist you with instruction. If you have access to one, you can use a projector to display what is on the computer screen onto a large screen. However, projectors can be very expensive, and your school may not have one that is easily accessible. Instead, you can use a video converter, which costs much less. A video converter connects the computer to a television or VCR. It displays what is on the teacher's computer monitor through the television for the entire class to see. For example, as you search for a topic on the Internet, the students can see the information and participate in a class discussion. You can use either video setup to demonstrate how to use new software programs. Teachers can also use multimedia software to model appropriate use of various strategies for students and colleagues (Brabec et al., 2004). Another example of how to use a single computer for group instruction is to project the agenda, content objectives, or lesson objectives for that particular class period onto the television or screen. Show the students what you expect them to accomplish during that class.

A single classroom computer can also be a benefit to students. It can be used as a student learning center where students can engage in reinforcement activities, individual practice, or assessments on concepts studied in class. One computer can also serve as a cooperative learning tool. It allows students to work together in small groups at the computer (Burkhart, 1998). You can also use software that poses real-life problems for the entire class to solve in cooperative groups. An example of such software is *Fizz and Martina's Math Adventures* from Tom Snyder Productions. Such software does not require all of the students to sit at the computer. Use a video converter or projector to display the program to the entire class and then direct the students to solve each problem at their desks, on the floor, or at tables in the classroom.

As you can see, no matter how many computers are in your classroom, computers and other technology can help you manage your classroom, accomplish administrative tasks, deliver instruction, and enhance student learning.

Chapter Six Reflection

1. How could you use a single computer (or a few computers) in your classroom?

   _____

   _____

   _____

   _____

   _____

2. Explain how you could provide equal computer or technology access to all of the students in your classroom.

   _____

   _____

   _____

   _____

   _____

3. Explain how you could use computers or other technology to assist you with at least five different classroom management tasks.

   _____

   _____

   _____

   _____

   _____

Computer Troubleshooting

Troubleshooting computer problems can be very frustrating. Consider that you are dealing with a machine that has multiple components simultaneously interacting with one another. It is often very difficult to pinpoint exactly which component of a particular device is creating the problem. Most teachers are not computer technicians. However, because of the influx of technology into education, it has become imperative that teachers learn some simple techniques to troubleshoot basic computer problems. Reading this chapter will help you fulfill the first section of NETS for teachers. Under the category of Technology Operations and Concepts, teachers should be able to "demonstrate introductory knowledge, skills, and understanding of concepts related to technology. . . (and) demonstrate continual growth in technology knowledge and skills to stay abreast of current and emerging technologies" (ISTE, 2002, p. 306). If you can solve various simple computer problems as they arise, you come closer to meeting these standards. Also, the people working in the district technology department tend to be very busy. If teachers can solve their own problems, student technology projects and technology-based learning can proceed much faster. Before you begin reading Chapter Seven, check your knowledge to see how much you already know about computer repair.

Check Your Knowledge

Directions: Evaluate the accuracy of each statement below. Place a T (for True) or an F (for False) in the space provided.

_____ 1. Input devices include a mouse, a scanner, a touch screen, and a keyboard.

_____ 2. Computer viruses can only be transmitted to your computer by accessing the Internet.

_____ 3. Malware and spyware are not harmful to your computer.

_____ 4. Rebooting the computer can often fix a computer or a software program that has become unresponsive.

_____ 5. All beeps that the computer makes signal a possible problem.

_____ 6. Computer technicians are the only individuals who should try to fix a computer problem.

_____ 7. Antivirus software will remove all viruses, spyware, and adware from the computer.

_____ 8. As long as you recognize the name of the person who sent you an email, you can open the email attachment without caution.

_____ 9. If your computer is connected to the school or district network, you may be limited in your authority to troubleshoot problems on your classroom computer(s).

_____ 10. If you are having computer problems, your first step should be to check and make sure that all of the cables and power cords are connected properly.

Computer Errors

A website devoted to writing at Colorado State University notes that computers are limited because they are programmed to work as they are told and that most computer problems are not actually the computer's fault. The website urges teachers in computer classrooms to learn about the capabilities of computers. Teachers need to practice using them, be patient, and use them as tools (CSU Dept. of English, 2006). Sometimes, a computer will alert you to a problem by displaying a message that indicates what is wrong. Often, you will be able to interpret the message and fix the problem. At other times, the language in the message will be too difficult to understand. Consult a fellow teacher or a computer technician when the computer error message is unfamiliar or too technical to interpret. The Microsoft website prompts that you may have to do some of your own "sleuthing," because each computer has a unique combination of hardware and software (Microsoft, 2004). Regardless of whether or not your computer displays a message, there are plenty of basic computer problems that any computer user can solve, and this section will describe some of these basic troubleshooting techniques. The Macintosh Apple website reminds us that, just like cars and toasters, computers need preventative maintenance to perform their best. Sometimes they can stop performing for no apparent reason, but there are often simple ways to take care of seemingly alarming issues (Apple, 2006).

A Word About Networks

School computers are usually networked within the building or within the district. This means that the documents or files created or accessed on one computer can be accessed on others within the network. The computers are connected through a server, and individual users of the network often log on using a network name and password.

When dealing with computer errors through a network system, it is important to note that the network administrator may have limited the amount of authority an individual user may have. Some of the suggestions listed below may not be applicable to your situation because of network security. Nonetheless, several of the tips listed below should be useful to you, and you are encouraged to try them to remedy easily-solved problems. Note however, if a problem cannot be resolved, you should contact a computer technician. You can find good online resources for support through many manufacturers who have "frequently asked questions" and knowledge-base articles (e.g., Microsoft.com and Apple.com). Type in "troubleshooting" in a search engine or the search text-box on the manufacturer website.

First Things First

There are several things that you can check to trouble-shoot a computer problem. Try the suggestions listed under each problem below:

1. **The computer won't turn on**—Make sure that everything is plugged in. Cables can come loose if the computer is moved or jostled. After checking the cables, if the computer still does not turn on, and you do not hear any noises coming from the system unit (i.e., the box containing the electronic components of the computer), this usually means that there is a problem with the power supply and it probably needs to be replaced.

2. **The mouse pointer will not move or you cannot type**—Reboot the computer. For PCs: use the CTRL-ALT-DEL keys to reboot a computer if it is completely frozen and not responding. You will need to hold the CTRL and the ALT keys at the same time and then tap the DEL (Delete) key. Release all of the keys at the same time. This will force the computer to reboot. For Macs: select

Restart, if possible. Try pushing Command-Q to start again. Sometimes Command-Option-Escape will force the computer to quit applications, along with selecting an application in a resulting window and clicking "Force Quit." You can also try to press the power button and click Restart when the dialog window appears. A last method, if nothing else works, is to unplug the power source and plug it in again. Make sure that the computer is booting from the hard drive and not a floppy disk. An error will occur if there is a floppy disk in the disk drive and you are trying to reboot the computer. If rebooting does not solve the problem, consult a computer technician.

3. **The software program is stalled (or frozen) or is not responding to your mouse clicks**—See if you can use your mouse in other open programs or on the desktop. If you can, then the problem is with the nonresponsive program. Try opening a new window for that program and resume working. If this is not feasible, end the nonresponsive program by pressing the CTRL-ALT-DEL keys (for PCs). The Windows Task Manager should appear. Select the program and click the End Task button. Now restart the program and continue working. If problems keep occurring, restart or reboot the computer. The Mac solutions for this problem are the same as when the mouse pointer will not move (see number two above).

4. **Can't connect to the Internet**—Check your modem or network cable connections. You will not be able to access the Internet if the cables are not completely connected.

5. **The computer gives a continuous beep at start up**—Check to see if something is lying on the mouse or keyboard and pressing down on one or more keys.

Onscreen Messages

As stated above, the computer will often display a message indicating what is wrong. Here is how to interpret these messages:

1. **Missing Operating System**—Somehow the computer's operating system has become corrupted. This could have happened because of a virus, a hard drive malfunction, or a computer user error. You will need to contact a computer technician. When using Macs, this type of error is indicated in any message containing "OS."

2. **Disk Boot Failure**—This error usually signifies that the hard drive has either become disconnected from the motherboard or is damaged. You will need to contact a computer technician. When using Macs, this type of error is apparent when the start up screen continually freezes or if a file folder with a blinking question mark appears.

3. **Keyboard Error or Locked**—Your keyboard is not plugged in properly. Turn off the computer, remove the keyboard from your computer, and connect the keyboard properly to your computer. Check to make sure that it is in the proper port on the back of the system unit. When using Macs, no error message will appear, the keyboard simply will not work.

4. **Nonsystem Disk or Disk Error**—You have accidentally left a floppy disk in drive A. Remove the disk from the drive and press any key on the keyboard. The computer will continue with the booting process. When using Macs, you may get a similar message if a peripheral device is connected incorrectly. Detach any new peripherals and restart.

Troubleshooting Input Devices

Input devices are devices that are connected to the computer and send data into the computer. Examples of input devices include keyboards and mice. Even though computer users rarely have problems with input devices, it is important to know how to troubleshoot them when they do happen, because you cannot operate a computer without certain key input devices such as a mouse and keyboard. Before you begin changing settings or installing and uninstalling drivers, there are some initial things that you can do:

1. **Loose connections**—Check to see if the input device is connected properly and securely. A loose connection and a bump of the computer can cause the cable to disconnect and cause the device to stop working.

2. **Computer viruses**—Check for viruses on the computer. You will need to run a virus scan using antivirus software.

The Mouse

1. **Clean the mouse**—If the mouse is not working properly, the problem could be the accumulation of dirt and dust from everyday use. The ball on the mechanical mouse can be removed for cleaning. (Note: optical mice do not contain small rubber balls.) The process consists of sliding or turning the disc that holds the mouse ball inside the mouse. The mouse ball will drop out when the mouse is turned right side up. There are three rollers inside the mouse ball cavity. It is important to remove all lint off of the rollers. That will allow the mouse pointer to move more freely.

2. **Mouse pointer movement**—If the computer mouse is not responding correctly, make sure that it is

on a flat surface and that the mouse rollers are clean. Another suggestion is to make sure that the mouse is plugged correctly into the mouse port on the back of the computer.

The Keyboard

1. **Constant beeping or clicking**—Not every beep signifies a problem, but if the computer is constantly beeping as it starts up, there may be a stuck key on the keyboard.

2. **Number pad on the keyboard**—If nothing happens when you press the number keys on the number pad (usually located on the right side of the keyboard), press the NUM LOCK key. If a small light (usually green) is lit, the NUM LOCK key is activated and the number keys on the number pad will work.

3. **Sticky keys on the keyboard**—When food or beverages are spilled on the keyboard, it can cause keys to stick. You can use compressed air made for cleaning keyboards. Office supply stores sell this "canned air," which contains a small straw for spraying into keyboard crevices.

Troubleshooting Output Devices

The Monitor

1. **The computer is on but the screen is blank**—Assuming that you have checked the screen controls (i.e., the brightness and contrast controls) and made sure that the monitor cable is properly connected to the system unit, the problem could be the video card or the monitor. If you have another monitor, substitute the faulty one with one that is known to be working. If the new one works, it means your original monitor is dead. If

the new monitor does not work, then it means the video card in the system unit is probably faulty and needs to be replaced.

2. **The screen is completely black**—If the computer screen is completely black, there are a couple possible solutions:

   - Check that the monitor cable is connected to the correct port on the back of the system unit and that the power cord is plugged into an electrical outlet.

   - Check the brightness setting of the computer. If it is on zero or on a low brightness setting, change the setting to a brighter setting.

3. **Monitor image is resized**—If the image on the computer monitor does not fill most of the screen, then the vertical or horizontal controls probably need to be adjusted. Use the controls on the monitor to do this. Start by finding the menu button. One of the options in the menu should be horizontal placement and another should be vertical placement (usually by pressing the menu button repeatedly, you can access the different options). Adjust the settings, as necessary, to size the image properly. If you make the necessary adjustments and the output does not change, then the monitor needs to be repaired or replaced.

The Desktop

1. **Working with the computer's desktop**—The computer background and icons on the computer screen are known as the computer's desktop. Occasionally, you can alter the desktop without realizing it. If you do not like the look of the desktop, change it. For PCs, the easiest way is to right-click anywhere on the desktop (but not on an icon) to bring up the desktop's shortcut

menu. To change the position of icons, choose "Arrange Icons" and select an option. To change the appearance of the desktop, select "Properties" and make the desired selections. For Macs, go to the APPLE menu (), then select "System Preferences" to change Desktop features.

2. **Adding desktop icons**—Desktop icons often need to be added, deleted, or organized on the computer's desktop. To modify desktop icons on a PC, right-click anywhere on the desktop. To add an icon, choose the "New" option and then click the "Shortcut" option. To complete the process, follow the computer's instructions. To delete an icon, right-click on the icon and select "Delete." When using a Mac, the process is slightly different. The desktop icon is called an *alias*. To create an alias, move the mouse pointer to the original program or application icon. Simultaneously hold down the "Option" and "Apple" keys and then drag the original icon to the desktop.

3. **The PC taskbar**—The PC taskbar is usually located at the bottom of the computer screen. It displays the Start menu and quick launch bar. The various icons and buttons are used to access and execute programs. The taskbar can be hidden or moved to another location on the screen.

   To hide the taskbar, move the mouse pointer to the top edge of the taskbar until a double-headed arrow appears. Press the left button on the mouse and drag the taskbar down to the very bottom of the screen. To make the taskbar reappear, move the mouse pointer to the bottom of the computer screen. When the double-headed arrow appears, hold the left mouse button and drag the task bar up toward the middle of the computer screen.

It is also possible to move the taskbar to either side of the screen or to the top of the computer screen. To relocate the taskbar, move the mouse pointer onto an open area of the taskbar. Hold down the left mouse button and drag the taskbar to the preferred location. Use the same process to move the taskbar back to the bottom of the computer screen.

4. **The Mac taskbar**—The Mac taskbar is known as the Dock. It contains a variety of applications that can be accessed quickly and easily. To customize or relocate the Dock, go to the APPLE menu and choose the Dock option. You will see a menu of options to choose from. When the dock is hidden, it is located at the bottom of the computer screen. When you move the mouse pointer to the bottom of the screen, it appears for immediate access, without remaining on the desktop as you work.

The Printer

1. **Printer won't turn on**—If the power light on the printer won't turn on, there are a few possible solutions:

    - Make sure that the power cord is plugged into an electrical outlet that is working properly.

    - Make sure that if the printer is plugged into a power strip that the power strip is turned on.

    - Make sure that no error lights are flashing on the printer. If an error light is flashing, the printer will not work.

2. **Printer is beeping**—If the printer is beeping, check to see if it is either out of paper or out of ink. If the paper and ink supplies are okay, then there is probably something wrong with the printer and it may need servicing.

3. **Printer won't print**—If a printer won't print, there are a few possible solutions:

   - Make sure that the printer has enough paper, ink, and toner.

   - Make sure that the printer cable is properly attached to the computer.

   - Run a "Test Print." Most printers have a built-in diagnostic program that will allow the printer to print a test page without communicating with a computer. The instructions for running a test print can be found in the printer owner's manual.

   - Make sure that there is no paper jamming the internal gears of the printer.

   - Make sure that the printer head of the inkjet printer is clean. Most inkjet printers have a utility that will clean the print head.

   - Make sure that the proper printer driver is installed on your computer. It is important that the printer driver that is installed is the correct driver for the printer that is connected to the computer. Unless you are familiar with printer drivers, consult your computer technician to install them.

   - If multiple printers are connected to the computer, make sure that you are printing to the correct printer. If you know how, check to see which printer is your computer's default printer.

   When using a Mac also try the following:

   - Select Print Monitor. Make sure that the document has completely spooled to the printer.

- Check in the Print Monitor to ensure that "Stop Printing" or "Stop Jobs" has not been selected. If it has, select "Start Printing" or "Start Jobs."

4. **When printing from a networked computer**—When a computer is networked, the administrator may have limited the control you have over what and where you can print. If you have exhausted the above suggestions, you may also want to try the following:

   - Check to make sure that the printer you are trying to print to is installed on the network. If it is, try reselecting and/or reinstalling it on your computer.

   - Select and print to a different printer. If you are able to print elsewhere, the printer is experiencing difficulty, not your computer.

   - Log onto a different computer on the network and try printing from it. If you are able to print now, this indicates a problem with how your computer is communicating with the printer.

5. **Paper won't stop coming out of the printer**—You can put an immediate stop to the paper by turning off the printer. However, you should also cancel the print job that is causing the problem. For PCs, open the Printer and Faxes panel (found in the Start menu) and double click the printer you are using. Select and delete the print job that is causing the problem. For Macs, choose "Show Jobs" from the printer menu and select "Stop Job" to delete the job.

The Speakers

1. **No sound from the speakers**—If you can't hear any sounds coming from the computer speakers, there are a few possible solutions:

   - Make sure that the power plug for the speakers is plugged into a working electrical outlet.
   - You will usually find three ports located on the sound card at the back of the computer. Make sure that the speakers are plugged into the proper port.
   - Try the speakers on another computer. If they work, then the sound card inside the computer is either loose or needs to be replaced.

2. **When using a Mac**—also try to select System Preferences under the APPLE menu. Check to make sure that the Mute box is not selected, that the correct output device is selected, and that the volume is turned up.

Prevent Common Computer Problems

File Management—It is very important to keep track of where you save files. It is not uncommon to create a file in September and then want to access it later in the school year, only to discover that it cannot be found. Or, you might receive an email that has an attachment. You save the file to the hard drive. A few days later, you try to access the file but are unable to locate it. A simple way to prevent these problems from occurring is to create folders that will store specific types of files. Teachers will often create a folder to hold just math files, a different folder to hold science files, and another folder to hold specific email attachments. To organize your files, you can create folders on the computer's desktop or inside other folders.

PC File Management—The steps to create a folder on a PC are the following:

- Open "My Computer" (from the Start menu or desktop) and determine where you want the new folder to be stored.

- Right click any "empty" or blank space in the active window or on the desktop and the shortcut menu should appear.

- Left click on "New" and on "Folder". The new folder will appear in the designated location. The text will be highlighted blue. You can now change the name of the folder.

Mac File Management—Adding a folder to a specific location on a Mac is a very similar process. It involves the following steps:

- Hold down the "Control" key and click the mouse button on any "empty" or blank space in an active window or on the desktop.

- Click on the "New Folder" option that appears in the menu.

- After the new folder appears, type the new folder name in the space. Drag the folder to the application in which you want it.

Data Files

Each time a person uses a software program to create a file, that file can only be opened by that specific program. The file contains certain codes that only the original program can read and understand. This can create problems when a person uses a software program on one computer that is not available on a second computer. When a person tries to open the data file, a few things can happen. First, the computer will display a message that the file cannot be opened or accessed. Secondly, the computer program will display a message that the file cannot be converted to the program's format. Lastly, the computer program will open the file, but the information is displayed as "hieroglyphics," or a variety of different characters that are all over the screen.

While some data files can never be opened by other programs, there are certain software applications that can open a variety of file formats. In addition, they allow the computer user to specifically save the data file in an alternative format. For example, you can write and save a letter in Microsoft Word, save it as a data file, and then later open and edit it in Corel WordPerfect.

The most common procedure for enabling data files to be accessed in multiple software applications is saving the initial data file in the format that is used by the other software program. To do this, select "Save As" from the File menu. After entering the file name, click on the down arrow next to the box that is labeled "Save File As Type." The dropdown box will display a list of different software applications that should be able to open the file that was just created. For example, if you will be opening a file later in Microsoft Works, then you need to access the "Save File As Type" box and save your file as a MS Works file. For Macs, select "Save As" from the File menu as well, but instead of choosing "Save File As Type," you will change the application under "Format." When you click on a specific application, a short description appears of the application changes that will occur.

Troubleshooting Viruses, Spyware, and Malware

Computer viruses are known to wreak havoc on computer systems. And, just like with humans, in order to get rid of the virus you have to know exactly what kind of virus it is. Viruses are considered an abuse of information. These attacks have cost the nation billions in security, maintenance, and lost productivity (Warlick, 2005). When the computer is infected with a virus, it can lose information, perform erratically, or become useless to the owner. "These abuses have forced information technology departments in our school districts to tighten down their networks, sometimes crippling our classroom technologies in terms of some of the best teaching and learning opportunities that it provides" (Warlick, 2005, p. 106).

Table 7.1 provides a list of categories and definitions that describe different types of computer viruses.

Table 7.1: Computer Virus Terminology

Type	Explanation
Adware	Advertisements that pop-up on your computer screen
Dialers	A program that alters your modem's setup so that it dials a 1-900 number and can potentially create a very large phone bill
Email virus	A virus that attaches itself to email messages in order to move from one computer to another
Hijackers	A program that takes control of your web browser and will direct you to only certain websites
Malware	Another name for malicious software. It is any kind of computer program that is designed to damage or interrupt a computer system. Examples of malware include viruses, adware, spyware, hijackers, toolbars, and dialers.
Spyware	A program that sends information about you and your computer to someone else. It can find and transmit email addresses, passwords, and even credit card information.
Toolbars	These attach themselves to Internet Explorer in order to enhance productivity. Examples include Google and Yahoo! toolbars. However, malware toolbars can actually take on the characteristics of adware, spyware, and hijackers.
Trojan horse	A computer program that states that it does one thing, yet it does another. For example, the program description states it is a computer game. However, once the program is run, it completely erases the hard drive of all of its data.
Virus	A small program that adheres itself to another program or file. Each time the file or program is accessed, the virus runs again, which can clog the computer's memory or destroy existing hardware or software.
Worm	A small program that moves around within a computer network making copies of itself

Protection from Viruses, Spyware, and Malware

1. **Antivirus software**—Viruses can be transmitted to your computer by accessing the Internet, opening email attachments, and installing programs or disk files with the virus attached. Therefore, you need to purchase an antivirus software program that allows for frequent updates. Norton AntiVirus and McAfee VirusScan are two of the most popular. There are free antivirus programs available on the Internet as well. However, do your research—if you are going to use a free program, you will

want to make sure that it will do the job! Most antivirus software programs will not remove spyware and adware from your computer.

2. **Antispyware and Antiadware software**—These programs will search your computer for any existing spyware and work to eliminate it from your computer. There are many free antispyware and antiadware programs available on the Internet. Most of them are free to the home user, but charge a fee to businesses and educational institutions.

3. **Update Often!**—It is very important to update antivirus, spyware, and adware software on a regular basis. It is actually suggested on a weekly basis. Some products can be set up to update whenever you log onto the Internet.

4. **Scan Often!**—Once you have updated your antivirus, spyware, and adware software, it is important to use the updated programs to scan your hard drive. After each program scans your hard drive, you will want to eliminate the infected files or programs, which will differ with each "anti" program.

5. **Be cautious about attachments**—Unless you are expecting an email attachment from a particular person, you should probably delete any emails that come with attachments. You should never open or run any unsolicited email attachments! Some viruses can even attach to an email address book and be sent out, so you need to be cautious even with emails from people you know.

6. **Backup**—It is important to back up any important information that you are saving on your hard drive. You can use floppy disks, CDs, or jump drives, depending on the size of the file or files. A backup of your files will give you a second copy in case something happens to the original files.

What Should the Teacher Do?— Problems

Below are some real-life technology problems that teachers face in educational settings. Try your best to solve each teacher's problem and then refer to page 176 for possible solutions.

1. A third-grade teacher, Mrs. Donner, decides to rearrange her classroom. She has just finished moving her computer to the other side of the room. She has reconnected all of the cables, but she is getting error messages that the keyboard and mouse will not work. What is the most likely cause of Mrs. Donner's problem?

   _____

   _____

   What suggestions would you make to fix the problem?

   _____

   _____

2. Mr. Willis, a seventh-grade teacher, is having problems with his mouse. As he tries to move the mouse across the screen, it is jumping erratically. What is most likely the cause of Mr. Willis' problem?

   _____

   _____

   What suggestions would you make to fix the problem?

   _____

   _____

3. A high school science teacher, Mrs. Bronsing, is at school and is trying to open a word processing file that she created at home. However, she cannot get the file to open. The computer keeps asking her which program she wants to use to open the file. Each time she selects a program, she gets "hieroglyphics" on the computer screen. What is most likely the cause of Mrs. Bronsing's problem?

   _____

   _____

   What suggestions would you make to fix the problem?

   _____

   _____

4. Mrs. Nykos, an elementary special education teacher, allowed some of her students to use her computer. At lunch, she wanted to check her email. However, the taskbar at the bottom of her screen had disappeared. What is most likely the cause of Mrs. Nykos' problem?

   _____

   _____

   What suggestions would you make to fix the problem?

   _____

   _____

What Should the Teacher Do?— Solutions

Problem 1:

Cause: The mouse and keyboard cables are in the wrong ports on the back of the computer system unit.

Suggestions: Mrs. Donner should look at the small pictures next to the ports on the back of the system unit. There is a specific port for the mouse and another one for the keyboard.

Problem 2:

Cause: The rollers in the mouse ball cavity are probably full of lint.

Suggestions: Mr. Willis needs to clean the lint off of the rollers using a fingernail or small brush.

Problem 3:

Cause: The file was probably created in a program that Mrs. Bronsing does not have on her school computer.

Suggestions: Mrs. Bronsing will need to locate a school computer that has the original program. She could also open the file on her home computer and then save the document in a format that is compatible with the computer programs at her school.

Problem 4:

Cause: The taskbar has been made smaller or has been hidden.

Suggestions: Mrs. Nykos should move her mouse around the edges of her computer screen. If the mouse pointer turns into a double-headed arrow, she should hold the left button on the mouse and drag the mouse to enlarge the taskbar. Another option is to move the mouse pointer around the screen to see if the taskbar appears and then disappears again. If this happens, Mrs. Nykos should right-click on the taskbar and uncheck the box that sets the taskbar to be hidden.

As you have learned in this chapter, there are many steps that you can take to troubleshoot computer problems. The problems are inevitable—your computer will not always work the way you would like it to. However, with just a few minutes of investigative work, you can solve many problems and quickly return to the task at hand.

Chapter Seven Reflection

1. How would you explain the importance of scanning your computer for viruses and spyware to your students and to your peers?

   _____

   _____

   _____

2. Why do you think that basic knowledge of computers and computer repair are a part of the ISTE NETS for teachers?

   _____

   _____

   _____

3. Why do you think that basic knowledge of computers and computer repair are a part of the ISTE NETS for students?

   _____

   _____

   _____

4. What are ways that you could share this information with other teachers at your school who are frustrated with the problems with their classroom computers?

   _____

   _____

   _____

Professional Development

Teachers need information, training, and guidance to guarantee that technology is benefiting student learning. Therefore, the goal for any effective technology professional development program should be to provide teachers with the opportunity to use the technology and to become familiar with ways in which to integrate technology into their classrooms.

There are several different components that can either make or break any professional development activity. When asked, most teachers will explain that a successful training session should easily relate to what the teacher is currently doing in his/her classroom, should fit into the teacher's schedule, should match the teacher's learning style, and that the outcomes of the training should be focused on the curriculum. The most difficult component is finding time in teachers' schedules for a workshop. Teachers are with students for at least six hours each day during the week. When not in the classroom, teachers are busy planning lessons, contacting parents, assessing students, and providing accommodations for children with special needs, among other tasks. Therefore, teachers often feel that there is not a lot of extra time to participate in professional development activities.

This chapter addresses that squeeze on teachers' time by highlighting a variety of professional development opportunities that might fit into your schedule. Some of the resources that will be discussed include networking with other educators, participating in professional organizations, reading professional magazines, and learning through online environments.

Check Your Knowledge

Directions: Evaluate the accuracy of each statement below. Place a T (for True) or an F (for False) in the space provided.

_____ 1. The sole purpose of professional development related to technology is to introduce the teacher to new forms of technology.

_____ 2. It is okay to ask a fellow teacher or a student how to complete a task using technology.

_____ 3. Professional organizations allow teachers to share their ideas with other educators.

_____ 4. Several magazine companies also have interactive websites that provide additional information to educators.

_____ 5. It is important for educators to stay current with technology-related issues by reading professional journals and magazines.

_____ 6. According to the International Society of Technology Educators (ISTE) website, there is a professional organization for teachers that focuses on technology in almost every state in the United States and in several other countries.

_____ 7. Even though most professional publications have a subscription fee, teachers can access the coordinating website to read about issues relating to technology in education.

_____ 8. Participating in online tutorials is a difficult and time-consuming process.

_____ 9. Knowing your learning style before you invest in professional development is not important.

_____ 10. It is possible to locate quality professional development opportunities that are free of charge.

Professional Development Opportunities

The ultimate value of professional development for teachers is the essential role that it plays in the improvement of student learning. While continued training is important for all areas of teaching and learning, it is especially important in the area of technology. Teachers not only have to develop new technology skills, but they must also learn how to integrate them into the curriculum. Teachers realize that they cannot effectively use or teach technology without the proper skills.

> The first step of any sound professional development program is to develop a belief about technology professional development that includes the idea that the curriculum drives the use of technology, not vice-versa, and that empowered teachers will find appropriate ways to include technology with their ongoing instruction rather than view it as an activity unconnected to the district's content standards. (Barnett, 2003, p. 2)

It would be ideal if school districts regularly provided or paid for technology professional development opportunities for all of their teachers. Sometimes, teachers in a school site will decide to form a professional development plan together. According to Harvey Barnett's research, in order for technology professional development to work well for teachers, principals must support the plan, teachers should be grouped by grade level and subject, and there must be time for hands-on activities. What does not work is top-down assertions without teacher input, lack of involvement from principals, little planning, one-hour workshops without follow-up, and a focus on software instead of using technology for curriculum (Barnett, 2003).

However, the school plan may not be realistic. Therefore, it is up to you to find your own technology-focused professional development. Before you determine what form of professional development you want to attempt, it is beneficial to examine your learning style. Do you want to be able to ask questions? Do you prefer to work at a self-directed pace? Do you like to read about a new product or concept and then investigate further on your own? After you have decided what form of training you would like to participate in, it is a good idea to review the advantages and disadvantages of each one. This way, you will feel comfortable taking part in the training.

You might also want to consider your expertise and comfort with computers. Researchers Mandinach and Cline identified fours stages of teachers learning about technology. A teacher at the *survival stage* resists technology, has unrealistic expectations, and only uses technology minimally in the classroom. A teacher at the *mastery stage* has increased tolerance and begins to use new ways to integrate technology with student interaction. These teachers troubleshoot simple computer problems. A teacher in the *impact stage* regularly uses technology in the classroom, balancing instruction with student activity in technology-based projects. A teacher in the *innovation stage* adapts the classroom environment to fully incorporate technology-enhanced curriculum and learning activities (Mandinach & Cline, 1992). The following paragraphs describe different types of professional development and the advantages and disadvantages of each one.

Face-to-Face Learning

The most basic form of professional development is to ask a friend, a fellow teacher, a technology leader, or even a student how to accomplish a specific technology-related task. Assuming that the person you ask has had prior experience using the specific hardware or software, this type of situation becomes a one-on-one tutoring session. It allows you to ask all kinds of questions without feeling illiterate. Quite often, without the opportunity of one-on-one learning, teachers shy away from using technology in their classrooms.

Another advantage to the peer-tutoring scenario is that the person who is labeled the "expert" gains interpersonal skills. This person learns to become a good listener and communicator and learns how to provide meaningful support to those seeking new skills. This person also gets the opportunity to improve and reflect upon personal technology skills. As the "expert" works with the teacher, he/she has to remember previous experiences and situations with the technology. By articulating certain steps or a process, the expert validates his/her own knowledge and skill level.

There are some disadvantages to face-to-face training. "Teachers are tired at the end of the day, and intense concentration can be difficult. The system works best to raise awareness, introduce concepts, or to learn about easy-to-use applications" (Barnett, 2003, p. 4). In one-on-one situations, participants miss out on hearing others' questions. They also miss out on receiving the input of others. However, in small or large training groups, participants have to share the instructor with others, have to work at the group's pace, and the training has to be scheduled at a time convenient for everyone.

Professional Organizations

One of the most renowned technology-related professional education organizations is the International Society for Technology in Education (ISTE). Over the years, it has become a driving force for the integration of technology into education. ISTE has affiliates for almost every state in the United States, as well as for a number of different countries. To locate the closest affiliate, contact ISTE through one of its publications or its website.

There are several advantages to joining a professional technology education organization. First of all, you have the opportunity to network with others who have the same interests, concerns, or questions that you do. Secondly, professional organizations usually offer a number of membership benefits. Most organizations have a professional publication that is mailed to members on a regular basis. They also often provide an electronic newsletter that is distributed on a more frequent basis. Thirdly, by joining a professional organization, you can receive discounts on merchandise or on memberships to affiliate organizations. Lastly, most professional organizations hold annual conferences. For a reasonable fee, you can participate in a one-day or multiple-day conference. A conference gives you the opportunity to interact with other educators from all over the city, state, or even country. By participating in the different events at the conference, you gain new ideas and new skills to bring to your classroom in order to improve student learning.

However, there can be disadvantages to relying on professional organizations for professional development. The membership fees can be expensive. You will need to travel to the organization's meetings, trainings, and conferences. Also, the meetings or trainings are not always scheduled at a time that is convenient for everyone.

Professional Publications

Since technology is forever changing, it is nearly impossible to stay abreast of all of the new and innovative ideas that are being implemented. Therefore, you must find a way to gain additional knowledge about what is happening in the area of educational technology. One of the easiest forms of professional development is to read professional magazines or ezines. There are several titles that focus specifically on education. Table 8.1 shows just a few of the professional technology publications available for educators.

Table 8.1: Professional Technology Publications

Magazine	Description	URL
Technology & Learning	A free magazine that has information about technology for educators, administrators, and technology leaders	**http://www.techlearning.com**
T.H.E. Journal	A free publication that focuses on providing information to educators about educational technology	**http://www.thejournal.com**
Educause	A nonprofit organization that provides information about technology-related professional development opportunities	**http://www.educause.edu**
Converge	An online magazine (ezine) that provides information to educators about grants, new products, and innovative ideas that incorporate technology	**http://www.convergemag.com**
eLearn	An ezine that provides information to teachers, administrators, and managers who are interested in offering online education opportunities	**http://www.elearnmag.org**
eSchool News	Provides information in both print and online to educators who are interested in educational technology issues that include legislation, court cases, new products, and grant opportunities	**http://www.eschoolnews.com**

With everything that educators are required to do on a daily basis, it is often difficult to find time to read professional journals or magazines. There are, however, several strategies for reading professional magazines more efficiently. First, glance at the table of contents and place a sticky note on the articles that you want to read at a later time. Next, make time to read by allowing yourself 30 minutes a day to read your professional journals or magazines. You will be able to skim through a lot of information by doing so. Lastly, after you have looked through a publication, rip out any articles that you want to reference at a later date or photocopy articles from magazines available at university libraries. Place the articles in a file folder or in an organized three-ring binder for future reference. This way, you do not hold on to magazines that you will never look at again or return to the library to reference them again. Also, when you find an article on the Internet that you want to read, print the article and then read it later. Again, place it in the file folder or three-ring binder that you have started for technology-related information.

There are a few disadvantages to professional publications. They do not provide interaction with others. You must seek out a fellow educator in order to discuss a particular article. One way to stimulate conversations on professional publications with others is to provide your principal with recommended readings that the entire staff reads and discusses during professional or staff meetings. Often, a professional publication covers a topic that happens to be related to an issue with which your school is dealing. Also, encourage your principal to subscribe to some of the major educational publications so that fees do not deter teachers from buying the publications and keeping up with current educational research.

Online Resources

With the schedules that educators keep, it is often difficult to attend after-school or Saturday workshops for professional development. Therefore, the Internet is a terrific place to turn for technology-focused professional development. Teachers receive "anytime, anywhere learning" where they can pick the time and location convenient to them for their professional development (Barnett, 2003).

First, there are two main modes of online professional development—synchronous and asynchronous courses. Synchronous courses are conducted in real time with the students and teacher connected via the Internet by videoconferencing or online written discussions (akin to a chat room). Asynchronous courses do not require the students and teacher to be online at the same time. Students access learning materials online and can post questions or responses to a discussion board on their own time.

The online professional development format has multiple advantages. First of all, it saves time. You do not have to drive to a workshop or class. For asynchronous courses, you can work on an online course at your convenience, maybe after school or at home late in the evening. Another advantage to online courses is that the information is up-to-date. As new hardware and software become available to educators, the correlating information, or tutorials, can easily be added to the Internet for immediate access by all those who are interested. One additional advantage is that there is an unlimited supply of professional development opportunities available on the Internet. For example, if you want to learn how to use Microsoft Word, you can perform a Google search and choose from multiple links. If, for some reason, your first choice does not offer the desired information, you can very easily select different tutorials until you find one that suits your interest.

However, when using online professional development, there are some disadvantages. Online courses often allow you to complete the work at your own pace, but this means you must be disciplined and commit yourself to completing the coursework. In addition, it may take several attempts to find an online training session that meets your needs. The description or the content of certain courses may not be what you are actually looking for.

Where Should You Start?

Because there are a multitude of professional development opportunities available to you, it is often difficult to determine what you should learn first. Since you can participate in online tutorials on just about every technology topic available, it is important for you to determine what project or task is the most important for you to accomplish. Do you need to create a classroom newsletter by Friday? Are you trying to set up a spreadsheet to monitor classroom expenses? Regardless of the task, the real question is, "Where should I start?"

No matter which type of professional development you choose, you will most likely find that the information you gain is useful. Utilization of professional resources is dependent largely upon you, your individual needs and learning styles, your time, and your availability. Table 8.2 on page 190 summarizes the methods covered within this chapter, as well as each method's advantages and disadvantages.

The main point of this chapter is to not wait for your school or district to schedule technology integration training for you. While formal training is most often very worthwhile, it is up to you to get the training you need to be a successful user and teacher of technology. As you can see from the options outlined in this chapter, there are many ways to expand your knowledge and skills in technology integration.

Table 8.2: Professional Development Strategy Summaries

Method	Advantages	Disadvantages
Face-to-Face and One-on-One Training	• Participant gets individual instruction • Participant is able to ask questions of instructor • Participant works at his/her own pace • Training can be scheduled at a time convenient for participant and instructor	• Participant misses out on others' questions and input
Face-to-Face Training in a Small or Large Group	• Participant hears the questions of other participants • Participant is able to ask questions of the instructor • Participant can get the input of others	• Participant shares the instructor with other participants • Participant works at a group pace • Training must be scheduled at a time convenient for the majority attending the training
Professional Organizations	• Participant can share ideas and concerns with individuals who have similar interests • Participant receives member benefits • Participant has option to attend conference(s) affiliated with organization	• Participants are usually charged membership fees • Meetings/trainings are usually scheduled at central locations • Meetings or trainings are not always scheduled at a time convenient for everyone
Professional Publications or Journals	• Several publications or journals are available free of charge • Publications can be read at a person's leisure • Articles can be removed from the publication and stored for later use • Subscriptions to publications can be ordered or stopped based on the person's current interests	• Provide no interaction with others • Several publications or journals cost money • Publications can be misplaced or never read • Ordered publications may not provide the information that a person is looking for
Online Training: Tutorials	• Training is self-directed • Training is self-paced • Participant can work on tutorial at any time and at any location • Many Internet tutorials are free of charge	• Participant has to be disciplined about completing the work • May have to read many course descriptions before finding what is needed
Online Training: Web-based Instruction	• Training can be self-directed • Training can be self-paced • Participant can work on assignments/training at any time and at any location • Participant can hold asynchronous and synchronous discussions with other participants • Participant can ask questions of the instructor	• Participant is usually charged a training fee or course fee • May have to read many course descriptions before finding what is needed

Chapter Eight Reflection

1. After reflecting on your learning style, explain which form of professional development would best meet your needs.

   _____

   _____

   _____

2. What major differences exist between the various forms of professional development opportunities?

   _____

   _____

   _____

3. What do you see as possible advantages of having so many different forms of professional development?

   _____

   _____

   _____

4. In the Brandywine School District, there are 176 teachers. The staff has been told that they must participate in some form of technology-based professional development within the next 60 days. How would you go about making suggestions to the teachers regarding the type of professional development in which they could participate?

   _____

   _____

   _____

Obtain Funding for Technology Integration

Do you have a lesson idea or project that involves technology, but you need extra money to bring it to fruition? Lack of school or district funds for educational projects is an ongoing stumbling block to teachers with exciting ideas. According to a National School Boards Association (NSBA) survey reported in 2005, funding for technology and incorporating technology into the classroom are among the leading challenges that school districts confront in the area of technology. Therefore, teachers must be creative when seeking funds for technology-related projects. However, if you take your time, search on the Internet, look through professional journals and magazines, and contact local businesses and foundations, you will most likely find a way to fund your project. "Having a well-conceived and descriptive technology plan is a critical factor for success when seeking technology funding" (Sun, Heath, Byrom, Phlegar, & Dimock, 2000, p. 215).

The focus of Chapter Nine is to explain the grant writing process. This includes how to prepare for a grant by collecting relevant data, where to find money to support a project, how to effectively write the standard eight components of the actual grant, and the important things that teachers need to remember as they work through and complete the grant writing process.

Check Your Knowledge

Directions: Evaluate the accuracy of each statement below. Place a T (for True) or an F (for False) in the space provided.

_____ 1. Grant administrators are interested in funding projects, not materials and equipment.

_____ 2. Including a project goal and multiple objectives in a grant application is optional.

_____ 3. The method explains the project sequence from start to finish.

_____ 4. There should always be a direct correlation between the project evaluation and the project goals and objectives.

_____ 5. The introduction is where you have the opportunity to describe your classroom, school, students, and community.

_____ 6. Statistics about the school, students, or classroom are included in the section with the project goals and objectives.

_____ 7. The components or criteria that are listed in the grant application are only suggestions.

_____ 8. If the grant proposal is rejected, it is always a good idea to ask the organization for a copy of the comments related to their decision.

_____ 9. A grant application has a better chance of being accepted if it is shown that it can be replicated in other situations or areas.

_____ 10. Grant proposals can stem from existing ideas to which a new twist or different component has been added.

What Is a Grant?

It is expensive to increase the amount of technology and technology education in a classroom, school building, or school district. Since many schools have tight budgets, the question becomes: Where are teachers or school administrators to find the money to fund additional technology-focused programs? The answer: grants.

So what exactly is a grant? It is an award of a specific amount of money to an individual or organization to finance a particular activity. It helps with specific costs involved in the implementation or continuation of a project.

Grant applications take planning and commitment. However, the potential payoff is that the grant money can help teachers or administrators provide outstanding educational opportunities for students.

Getting Started

To get the grant process started, come up with an idea for the grant proposal. While preparing the documentation can be time-consuming, the more planning and preparation you do, the more successful you will be in acquiring the funding, especially if you already have a well-organized technology plan (Sun et al., 2000). It is important to expand your proposal beyond acquiring technology; grant funders want to support projects that focus on improving student learning or on research-based solutions. Even if the goal is professional development, the eventual end needs to demonstrate that it will affect student success (Rivero, 2004). Brainstorm with individuals who will benefit from the project to generate ideas for a potentially better grant project.

However, it is not enough to have a good idea. Good planning is essential to the proposal's success. In addition to brainstorming, research the feasibility of the project. A few questions to ask during this process are:

- What do you want to do, how much will it cost, and how much time will it take?

- What difference will the project make for students or the learning process?

- What has already been done in the area of your project? By whom? What were the results?

- How does the project fit within the curriculum?

- Is the project focused on one classroom, or can it be replicated throughout the entire school or in other schools?

- How will you accomplish your project? What is your plan of attack?

- How will the success of the project be evaluated?

- How will the project be maintained once it is implemented?

Finding the Money

Once you have a grant proposal in mind, you need to find the appropriate funder. There are two main sources for funding—the public and private sectors. Public funders are usually organizations at the state or federal level. The grants that they offer are very competitive and have more complex requirements than other grant programs. They tend to fund large-scale projects, which are usually geared toward school districts rather than individual teachers. Public grants may require partnerships with other institutions (e.g., libraries, museums, or community organizations). Typically, public grants have only one deadline per year.

Private funders are foundations and corporations. They are private entities, usually not-for-profits, set up for the sole purpose of giving away money to support certain goals or projects. Private funders are excellent sources of funding for individual classroom projects. They tend to offer dollar amounts that are more appropriate for classroom projects than for projects at the district level. The grant proposal process can be much simpler, and there are often multiple deadlines each year. There are several places to look to find just the right private funder. Start by looking at the following:

- District educational foundations

- Top ten employers in the community

- Technology vendors

- Websites such as The Foundation Center

As you look for a funder for your project, it is important to review the eligibility requirements. Funders are very specific about what they will and will not fund. For this reason, it is important that you contact them for more information. Keep in mind that there is nothing wrong with asking the funder for suggestions as to how to enhance your application! It is important to figure out the cost of each component in the total plan so that you can know where to cut back if the whole project is not funded (Sun et al., 2000). Also, consider the amount of award money each organization is willing to give. This will determine if you need to submit several proposals to multiple organizations in order to cover the costs of the project. Districts can create three- to five-year plans and implement various phases, which is important if you are not able to get funding for each component of your technology plan (Sun et al.). Finally, it is very important to consider the grant deadline. It takes time to write a successful grant. It is not something that can be done in a week.

Writing the Proposal

There are several components to a proposal:

- Proposal summary (or abstract)
- Introduction of the organization seeking funds
- Problem statement (or needs assessment)
- Project objectives or description
- Project methods or design
- Project evaluation
- Project budget

Proposal Summary

The proposal summary outlines the proposed grant project. It should include brief statements that explain the problem, the solution, the funding requirements, and information about the people involved with the project. Depending on the funder's requirements, the proposal summary could be a cover letter or the initial page of the proposal. Regardless of its location, it should be brief, no more than two or three paragraphs, or about 250–500 words. Oftentimes, the summary is written after the grant proposal has been developed, to ensure that all the key points of the project are included. The proposal summary becomes the foundation of your proposal. It gives the grant reader a first impression of the project. In many cases, the summary is the most carefully scrutinized and reviewed part of the grant application.

Introduction

The introduction is the place in the grant proposal to share information about your classroom, the students, the school, and the community. The introduction could also be called "Statement of Need." This section enables the reader to learn more about the problem that you and your students face. It presents the necessary facts and evidence that support the need for the grant project. It helps to establish that you recognize the problem and are willing to work to find a solution. The information or statistics that are used in this section can come from building- or district-wide sources or from your classroom observations.

The Problem Statement

The problem statement explains the need or the purpose of the project. It needs to be supported with evidence that stems from specific experiences or statistics from reliable sources. It is important to stay focused on the project's purpose and describe the present problem.

The Project Description

The project description should include the goal(s) and objectives of the grant project. "Good goals are at the core of all good proposals" (Sun et al., 2000, p. 220). The goal states the purpose of the project. The objectives are the measurable outcomes of the grant project. They specify concretely how the project will improve student learning. It is not enough to say you just want to buy things because you do not have them; you must explain how the technology will act as a tool for improving the learning environment (Rivero, 2004).

As you consider how to write the objectives for the grant project, it is important to remember that there are four different types of objectives: behavioral, performance, process, and product. A behavioral objective focuses on what the student or teacher does. A performance objective pertains to an expected level of proficiency after the project is complete. The process objective refers to how the grant project will be documented as it progresses. The product objective states or describes the final product that is generated by the project.

The Method

The method section is where the project components are detailed. It describes the how, the when, and the why of the grant project. You need to describe how the project will progress from start to finish, when each component of the grant project takes place, how the project will be staffed, and why the project is significant enough to make a difference in student learning. Most funders also want to know how you will sustain the project after funding runs out, so be sure to include this explanation.

The Evaluation

The evaluation component of the grant application explains how the project will be evaluated. It should also explain the method that will be used to evaluate the project and who will be doing the evaluation. Funders are interested in technology plans that measure success, identify possible problems, and ask questions for future research (Sun et al., 2000). In addition, this section must show a direct correlation between the evaluation process and the goals and objectives that were described earlier.

The Budget

The budget section of the grant application has several purposes. It is used to explain the project from a monetary standpoint. It should contain an itemized list of all funds needed for the project, an itemized list of items and funds that have been supplied by the school or teacher, and an itemized plan for future funding. It is important to remember that the budget is not just an accounting of possible expenses, but it is also a way for the grant seeker to describe the project in monetary terms. Most importantly, the budget should relate all of the project costs with the project objectives in dollars and cents. Do not round numbers up or down. It is also important to clearly explain how the budgeted items were calculated.

Things to Remember

As you work through the grant writing process, there are several things that you should remember. First of all, do not become discouraged if you receive a rejection from a possible funding source. In most cases, there are large numbers of people applying for each grant that is available, and the funders have only so much money. Therefore, just because the grant is turned down, it does not mean that it is poorly written or not worthwhile. Sometimes, you can obtain the reader's comments and resubmit with success accruing to the remarks made (Rivero, 2004).

Second, it is very important to read the funder's guidelines and instructions carefully. The closer you follow the directions and the presentation requirements, the higher your chances of qualifying for funding (Rivero, 2004). Make sure that no steps are skipped. If you read the Request for Proposal (RFP) carefully, you will not waste valuable time (yours and theirs) by submitting a proposal that does not meet the funding requirements (Sun et al., 2000). Because the funders are giving away their money, they have the right to determine exactly what information they want to ask in the grant application. It is also essential that you do not try to make the funder's program fit your project. Your project must be in line with the funding agency's priorities and expectations.

Third, the project and all of its components should be innovative, creative, and educational. Funders want to give money to projects that are unique and show a lot of forethought. That does not necessarily mean that the grant project has to be a new idea. There is nothing wrong with taking an existing idea and altering it to meet the needs of a different grant or application. Note that funders, public or private, will rarely fund construction or existing operating expenses. They want to fund the projects that will make a difference in a specific area of interest. For the most part, they usually invest in supplemental programs. Private foundations often seek creative solutions to problems/needs, but they usually do not wish to fund risky projects. It is important to keep your ideas and goals realistic. It is very easy to come up with a far-out or really awesome idea for a grant project; however, if the project or the goals and objectives that are written for the project are too extreme, it is very possible that the grant request will not be funded.

Fourth, it is very important to have an evaluation plan. Funders want to know if the projects they fund will be successful. They want to know if the project is meeting its goals and your proposal should include how you will determine its success.

Fifth, make sure that your project is replicable. The funder wants to know that the grant project can be duplicated in other locations or situations. Explain how the project can be extended to other grades or schools.

Sixth, have a reasonable, detailed budget. It is extremely important to do the necessary research on all costs associated with the project prior to submitting the application. It is also very important to explain the budget even if there are no requirements to do so. There should never be any doubt or concern with regard to the budget.

Lastly, proofreading is one of the most important steps in the grant writing process. Spelling and grammar errors do not convey a positive image. The funders are relying on the grant proposal as the first impression. If the application is poorly written or has multiple mistakes, it tends to give the impression that it was slapped together or written in a hurry. Also, never use abbreviations or educational lingo that a "non-teacher" would not understand. Most grant reviewers are not educators. If possible, have a friend or family member who is not an educator read the grant application to look for education lingo. Even the term *cooperative learning* is not well-known outside of the education profession.

Obtaining grants can make your educational projects possible. Do not let your classroom budget limit you. You can bring unique learning opportunities to your students, boost your school's profile, and inspire other teachers to dream a little bigger by your example.

Chapter Nine Reflection

1. Explain the importance of following all of the directions on a grant application.

   _____

   _____

   _____

2. Ballard Elementary wants to install a community technology lab in its school. The teachers write a grant asking for assistance with buying computers, software, wire, cables, tables, chairs, and other components needed for the setup. The grant proposal also asks for assistance with electric bills, Internet access, and a coordinator's salary. Explain why you believe the grant proposal either will or will not be funded.

   _____

   _____

   _____

3. After reviewing the seven different components to a standard grant application, determine which one is the most important. Explain your reasoning.

   _____

   _____

   _____

4. Using one of the grant resources from this chapter or one of your own, find a grant opportunity that interests you. Explain why this grant is applicable to your classroom.

   _____

   _____

   _____

Appendix A: Resources for Students

Kids Search Engines—Search "kids search engines" for current resources; here are some examples of popular kid-friendly search engines:

- **Ask For Kids** (http://www.askforkids.com)
- **KidsClick** (http://www.kidsclick.org)
- **Yahooligans!** (http://www.yahooligans.com)
- **CyberSleuth Kids** (http://cybersleuth-kids.com)
- **American Library Association's Great Websites for Kids** (http://www.ala.org/greatsites)
- **First Gov for Kids** (http://www.kids.gov)
- **AOL at School** (http://www.aolatschool.com/students)

Resources for Scientific Research—Search "science research for kids" to find science research opportunities for students. Here are the resources for scientific research provided in this book:

- **The GLOBE Program** (http://www.globe.gov)
- **The JASON Project** (http://www.jasonproject.org)
- **Global Lab Curriculum** (http://globallab.terc.edu)
- **Center for Innovation in Engineering and Science Education** (http://www.ciese.org)

Resources for Internet Exchange Projects—Search for "internet exchange projects," "K–12 email exchange projects," or "internet exchange projects for kids" to see what results you get. Here are some examples of current internet exchange project opportunities:

- **Global SchoolNet Internet Projects Registry** (http://www.globalschoolnet.org)
- **Flat Stanley Project** (http://www.flatstanley.com)
- **Global Virtual Classroom** (http://www.virtualclassroom.org)

Appendix B: Rubric Resources for Teachers

The free resources listed below offer, in addition to rubrics, a range of downloadable materials including graphic organizers, lesson plans, calendars, and articles, as well as links to other sites. You could also search for "rubrics" in a search engine to find additional resources.

Name of Web Resource	Description	URL
Discovery School's Kathy Schrock's Guide for Educators	Provides an extensive bank of subject-specific and general rubrics, in addition to articles about assessment issues and links to other online rubric banks and generators.	**http://school.discovery.com/ schrockguide/assess.html**
Tech4Learning (Recipes for Success)	Provides Rubric Maker, a rubric generator, that offers customizable templates with many features including various rubric elements, categories for primary, elementary, and high school topics, suggested language, editing guidelines, and product options. When you go to the main page, click on "Tools."	**http://www.myt4l.com**
Rubrics 4 Teachers	Provides example rubrics and rubric-related information available in downloadable pdf files, as well as links to other teacher resources.	**http://www.rubrics4teachers.com**

"Check Your Knowledge" Answer Key

Chapter One (page 12)

1. F
2. T
3. T
4. T
5. F
6. F
7. T
8. T
9. T
10. T

Chapter Two (page 32)

1. T
2. T
3. T
4. T
5. F
6. T
7. F
8. F
9. F
10. F

Chapter Three (page 57)

1. T
2. T
3. F
4. F
5. T

6. T
7. F
8. T
9. T
10. F

Chapter Four (page 91)

1. F
2. T
3. T
4. F
5. F
6. T
7. F
8. T
9. F
10. T

Chapter Five (page 123)

1. F
2. T
3. T
4. T
5. F
6. T
7. T
8. T
9. T
10. T

"Check Your Knowledge" Answer Key *(cont.)*

Chapter Six (page 140)

1. F
2. F
3. T
4. T
5. T
6. T
7. T
8. F
9. T
10. T

Chapter Eight (page 181)

1. F
2. T
3. T
4. T
5. T
6. T
7. T
8. F
9. F
10. T

Chapter Seven (page 156)

1. T
2. F
3. F
4. T
5. F
6. F
7. F
8. F
9. T
10. T

Chapter Nine (page 195)

1. T
2. F
3. T
4. T
5. T
6. F
7. F
8. T
9. T
10. T

Glossary

Acceptable Use Policy—a document with rules that a computer user must agree to follow in order to have access to a network or to the Internet

adware—advertising banners that appear on the computer screen when accessing the Internet

antivirus software—software that searches storage devices for any types of viruses

application—a computer program that is designed to help a user accomplish specific tasks

attachment—a file that is attached to an email; the email and file are received at the same time

back up—to copy important data onto a separate storage device for safety

bookmark—a URL that is stored for easy retrieval at a later date

browser—a computer program used to navigate the Web

chat room—an online location where individuals communicate in real time

clip art—images, cartoons, or graphics that are used to enhance a document

component—a piece of computer hardware that is a part of the total system

compressing files—compacting files to make them smaller in order to save space

database—a collection of data that is organized into headings, fields, and records

default—the original format or settings, usually determined by the manufacturer and set up automatically during installation

desktop publishing—the software and/or the process that gives the user complete control over the design, page layout, or format of a document

device driver—a small program that helps an attached device communicate with the computer system

document—a file that is created on a computer and can be printed on paper

download—the process of transferring data from another computer "down" to your computer

email—text messages that are sent over the Internet

ePortfolio—an electronic portfolio; a variety of digital and multimedia files that are combined into one folder in order to share information about a topic or person

export—to send a file from your computer; to send out a file from a specific software program

field—a category of information in a database file

file—information that is stored under one name so that it can be accessed by a specific software program

file management—the organizing of files on a storage device into different folders

font—letters, numbers, and symbols that represent one particular design of a set of characters

graphics—images or clip art that are used to enhance various documents

hardware—the electronic components of a computer system

hits—the number of results that appear when doing a search using a search engine

hotlists—a list of popular or specific websites that have a similar theme; often created by teachers to expedite Internet searching by students

import—to bring a file into your computer or into a specific software program

input device—computer hardware that is used to send information into a computer, i.e., keyboard, mouse, or touch screen

instant message—the exchange of messages in real time between two or more people

Interactive Response System—remotes that send student responses to teacher questions to a receiver and are electronically recorded

jump drive—a portable USB storage device

listservs—a program that maintains a list of email addresses and sends a single email message to all email addresses

load—to install software on the computer hard drive

malware—malicious software that can damage a computer system, e.g., viruses, spyware, and worms

modem—a hardware device that allows a computer to communicate with other computers over a phone line or other lines that transmit data, e.g., cable and DSL

monitor—the computer screen that allows you to see the information that the computer is manipulating; an output device

motherboard—the main circuit board of the computer system

mouse—an input device that helps the computer user to maneuver around a computer screen and in software programs

multimedia—using text, graphics, animation, audio, and video files to create a presentation

netiquette—the rules of conduct on the Internet; acting in ways that do not anger or frustrate others while online

NETS—National Education Technology Standards; standards developed by the International Society of Technology in Education (ISTE)

network cable—a wire that connects a computer to the local area network

online—the state of the connection of the computer to the network or to the Internet

operating system—the main software program that communicates with the computer hardware and software in order to process various tasks

output device—a hardware device that shows information that comes from a computer, e.g., monitor, screen, video projector, or printer

PDF file—Portable Document Format; a file that duplicates the format and information of a document, regardless of the software program, to a read-only document

peripheral device—an external device that is added onto a standard computer system, e.g., printer, mouse, and modem

port—a place on a computer where devices (e.g., keyboard, mouse, printer, digital camera) are connected, usually in the back

printer driver—the software program that provides communication between the printer and the computer

printer head—the part of an inkjet printer that moves back and forth as it sprays the paper with thousands of dots of ink

query—a search for information using a specific criteria

reboot—to restart the computer

record—all of the fields or categories of information about one item in a database

reinstall—to repeat the installation process of a program; usually done when an error occurs with the program

rubric—evaluation tool that specifies criteria for each level of proficiency

scan—to convert the printed page to a digital image or lines of text

scanner—the hardware that reads the printed page and converts it to a digital image or lines of text

settings—how the device is set up or configured to respond

software—the instructions for the computer; a computer program

sound card—a circuit board that plugs into a slot inside the computer to enhance sound files (wav, midi, etc.); records and plays back sounds; has a port that allows for input from a microphone

spyware—a computer program that shares information about the user's Internet access with a specific website; program runs "behind the scenes"

system unit—the box and its contents which are the motherboard and other electronic components of the computer; also called a CPU (Central Processing Unit)

taskbar—a toolbar that shows the active or open applications; usually located at the bottom of the computer screen

technology—a device that is used to solve a problem; usually electronic in nature

technology performance profiles—benchmarks that describe the skills that students and teachers should have at various levels of education

templates—a document that is predesigned or formatted to help save time when creating a new document

touch screen—a screen that is sensitive to the touch; special computer monitors or displays

uninstall—to remove a software program from a computer

upload—to send a file from your computer to another computer or device

URL—Universal Resource Locator; the specific address or location of a website or Web page on the Internet

USB—Universal Serial Bus; a type of connector used to connect one device to another, e.g., printer to computer, jump drive to computer, mouse to system unit

video projector—an output device that projects an image from the computer onto a wall size screen; data projector

virus—software that infects or damages a computer; can affect the hardware and/or the software of the computer

Web browser—a program that allows you to view a Web page from the Internet on your computer

Web search—searching the World Wide Web or the Internet for information

Weblogs—a list of postings or messages on a Web page that focus on a particular topic; can contain editorials, comments, images, or creative writings; also known as Web logs or blogs

WebQuest—the process of searching the Internet for specific information or clues about a specific topic; used by educators as Internet projects for students and classes

WYSIWYG—"What You See Is What You Get"; the way the document looks on the computer screen is how it will look when it is printed on paper

zip files— files that have been compressed or made smaller in size

References

Apple Computer, Inc. (1995). *Changing the conversation about teaching learning and technology: A report on 10 years of ACOT research.* Cupertino, CA: Apple Computer, Inc. Retrieved June 26, 2006, from http://images.apple.com/education/k12/leadership/acot/pdf/10yr.pdf

Apple Computer, Inc. (2006). *Mac 101: Get started with the Mac.* Retrieved August 12, 2006, from http://www.apple.com/support/mac101/

Apple Works: Simple projects (primary). (2003). Huntington Beach, CA: Teacher Created Materials.

Ascione, L. (Ed.). (2005, September 1). Teachers' tech use on the rise. *eSchool News Online.* Retrieved July 2, 2006, from http://www.eschoolnews.com/news/showStory.cfm?ArticleID=5839

Balser, E. (2001). Integrating technology into courses for pre-service teachers. In C. Crawford, D. A. Willis, R. Carlsen, I. Gibson, K. McFerrin, J. Price, & R. Weber (Eds.), *Proceedings of Society for Information Technology and Teacher International Conference* (pp. 1534–1539). Chesapeake, VA: Association for the Advancement of Computing in Education.

Barnett, H. (2003). *Technology professional development: Successful strategies for teacher change.* Syracuse, NY: ERIC Clearinghouse on Information and Technology. (Eric Document Reproduction Service No. ED477616)

Brabec, K., Fisher, K., & Pitler, H. (2004). Building better instruction: How technology supports nine research-proven instructional strategies. *Learning and Leading with Technology, 31(5),* 6–11.

Burkhart, L. (1998). *Tip sheet: Classroom management.* Retrieved July 15, 2005, from http://www.lburkhart.com/elem/tip4.htm

CEO Forum on Education and Technology. (2001). *Education technology must be included in comprehensive education legislation.* Washington, DC: The CEO Forum on Education and Technology. (ERIC Document Reproduction Service No. ED456822).

Chard, S., & Katz, L. (2001). *Project approach in early childhood and elementary education.* Retrieved July 10, 2006, from http://www.project-approach.com/default.htm

Colorado State University Department of English. (2006). *Computers can only count to one.* Retrieved August 11, 2006, from the Writing @ CSU Website: http://writing.colostate.edu/guides/teaching/pcclass/pop7b.cfm

Dodge, B. (1997). *Some thoughts about WebQuests.* Retrieved July 1, 2006, from the WebQuest Page, San Diego State University: http://webquest.sdsu.edu/about_webquests.html

Eisenberg, M. B., & Johnson, D. (2002). *Learning and teaching information technology—Computer skills in context.* Syracuse, NY: ERIC Clearinghouse on Information and Technology. (ERIC Document Reproduction Service No. ED465377)

Ellis, K. (2002). *New technologies link ancient cultures.* Retrieved August 7, 2006, from Edutopia, the George Lucas Educational Foundation Website: http://www.edutopia.org/php/article.php?id=Art_979&key=037

Forrest, D., & Forrest, M. (2001). *Becoming an accomplished teacher in the 21st century.* Retrieved July 7, 2006, from Edutopia, the George Lucas Educational Foundation Website: http://www.edutopia.org/php/article.php?id=Art_737

Fryer, W. A. (2001, Winter). An excel shortcourse for teachers. *TechEdge*, 16–19. Retrieved July 20, 2006, from http://www.tcea.org/Publications/Excel.pdf

Furger, R. (2002, Spring). From Spearfish to Sakaide City: A teacher's odyssey. *Edutopia Newsletter*, 4–5. Retrieved August 7, 2006, from http://www.edutopia.org/EdutopiaPDF/Spring02.pdf

Goodrich, H. (1996, December/1997, January). Understanding rubrics. *Educational Leadership 54(4)*, 14–17.

Graham, D., & Mason, D. (2000, March 1). *Multimedia applications on a shoestring budget.* Retrieved June 15, 2005, from http://www.techlearning.com/db_area/archives/WCE/archives/donnas.htm

Hawkins, J. (1997). The world at your fingertips. In P. Burness & W. Snider (Eds.), *Live & Learn* (pp. 213–215). Nicasio, CA: The George Lucas Educational Foundation.

Hobbs, R. (2006). Multiple visions of multimedia literacy: Emerging areas of synthesis. In M. C. McKenna, L. D. Labbo, R. D. Kieffer, & D. Reinking (Eds), *International Handbook of Literacy and Technology* (Vol. II, pp. 15–28). Mahwah, NJ: Lawrence Erlbaum Associates.

Holum, A., & Gahala, J. (2001). *Using technology to enhance literacy instruction* (Critical Issue). Naperville, IL: North Central Regional Educational Laboratory. Retrieved November 19, 2005, from http://www.ncrel.org/sdrs/areas/issues/content/cntareas/reading/li300.htm

Information literacy in an information society. (1994). Syracuse, NY: ERIC Clearinghouse on Information and Technology. (ERIC Document Reproduction Service No. ED372756)

International Society for Technology in Education. (2000). *National educational technology standards for students: Connecting curriculum and technology*. Eugene, OR: ISTE Publications.

International Society for Technology in Education. (2002). *National educational technology standards for teachers: Preparing teachers to use technology*. Eugene, OR: ISTE Publications.

Jay, M. E. (2006). *Information literacy: Unlocking your child's door to the world*. Chicago: American Library Association. Retrieved July 10, 2006, from http://www.ala.org/ala/aasl/schlibrariesandyou/parentsandcomm/informationliteracy.htm

Kulik, J. A. (2003). *Effects of using instructional technology in elementary and secondary schools: What controlled evaluation studies say* (SRI Project No. P10446.001). Arlington, VA: SRI International.

Lamb, A. (2005). *Evaluating internet resources*. Retrieved April 11, 2005, from http://eduscapes.com/tap/topic32.htm

Mandinach, E., & Cline, H. (1992, April). *The impact of technological curriculum innovation on teaching and learning activities*. Paper presented at the annual conference of the American Educational Research Association, San Francisco, CA.

McKenzie, J. (1998, March). Creating technology enhanced student-centered learning environments. *From Now On: The Educational Technology Journal, 7(6)*. Retrieved July 19, 2006, from http://www.fromnowon.org/mar98/flotilla.html

McKenzie, J. (2000). *Beyond technology: Questioning, research and the information literate school*. Bellingham, WA: FNO Press.

Means, B., Blando, J., Olson, K., Middleton, T., Morocco, C. C., Remz, A. R., & Zorfas, J. (1993). *Using technology to support education reform*. Washington, DC: U.S. Government Printing Office.

Means, B., & Olson, K. (1994). The link between technology and authentic learning. *Educational Leadership, 51(7)*, 15–18.

Microsft Corporation. (2004). *Using and maintaining your network.* Retrieved August 12, 2006, from http://www.microsoft.com/windowsxp/using/networking/maintain/default.mspx

Moursund, D., & Smith, I. (2000). *Research on technology in education.* Retrieved July 12, 2006, from International Society for Technology in Education Website: http://www.iste.org/Content/NavigationMenu/Research/Reports/ISTE_Research_Reports.htm

National School Boards Association. (2005). *Technology survey reveals funding and integration into classroom biggest challenges; Preparedness of new teachers also a concern.* Retrieved August 5, 2006, from the NSBA Website: http://www.nsba.org/site/doc.asp?TRACKID=&VID=2&CID=1591&DID=37031

Norman, K. I., & Hayden, K. L. (2002, July/August). K–12 instruction in the United States: Integrating national standards for science and writing through emerging technologies. In N. Bizzo, C. S. Kawaski, L. Ferracioli, & V. Leyser da Rosa (Eds.), *Rethinking science and technology education to meet the demands of future generations in a changing world* (pp. 323–333). Proceedings of the 10th IOSTE Symposium, Foz do Iguaçú, Brazil.

Parsad, B., & Jones, J. (2005). *Internet access in U.S. public schools and classrooms: 1994–2003* (NCES 2005015). Washington, DC: National Center for Education Statistics.

Penuel, B., Golan, S., Means, B., & Korbak, C. (2000). *Silicon Valley challenge 2000: Year 4 report.* Menlo Park, CA: SRI International.

Reeves, T. C. (1998). *The impact of media and technology in schools: A research report prepared for the Bertelsmann Foundation.* Athens: The University of Georgia. Retrieved July 10, 2006, from http://itech1.coe.uga.edu/~treeves/edit6900/BertelsmannReeves98.pdf

Rivero, V. (2004, September/October). Money (that's what I want): Scoop up those elusive grant dollars. *Edutopia 1(1)*, 24.

Roschelle, J., Pea, R., Hoadley, C., Gordin, D., & Means, B. (2001). Changing what and how children learn in school with computer-based technologies. *The Future of Children 10(2)*, 76–101.

Sandholtz, J. H., Ringstaff, C., & Dwyer, D. C. (1997). *Teaching with technology: Creating student-centered classrooms.* New York: Teachers College Press.

Silverstein, G., Frechtling, J., & Miyaoka, A. (2000). *Evaluation of the use of technology in Illinois public schools: Final report.* Rockville, MD: Westat.

Stiggins, R. (1997). *Student-centered classroom assessment* (2nd ed.). Upper Saddle River, NJ: Prentice-Hall.

Sun, J., Heath, M., Byrom, E., Phlegar, J., & Dimock, K. V. (2000). *Planning into practice: Resources for planning, implementing, and integrating instructional technology.* Durham, NC: South East and Islands Regional Technology in Education Consortium.

Tapscott, D. (1998). *Growing up digital: The rise of the Net generation.* New York: McGraw-Hill.

Teachnology, Inc. (2006). *PowerPoint in the classroom.* Retrieved November 22, 2005, from http://www.teach-nology.com/tutorials/powerpoint/print.htm

TechTools: Resource kit for Microsoft PowerPoint. (2003). Huntington Beach, CA: Teacher Created Materials.

Thornburg, D. (2002, December). *Applying technology to assess student learning.* Retrieved July 5, 2006, from the PBS TeacherLine Website: http://teacherline.pbs.org/teacherline/resources/thornburg/thornburg1202.cfm

Tousignant, M. (Ed.). (1996). *Ideas for the one computer classroom.* Madison, WI: Madison Metropolitan School District. Retrieved November 19, 2005, http://danenet.wicip.org/mmsd-it/tlc/1comprm.html

Warlick, D. F. (2005). *Raw materials for the mind: Information, technology, and teaching & learning in the twenty-first century* (4th ed). Raleigh, NC: The Landmark Project.

Wellington, Y. (1998, Summer). Assistive technology success stories. *Edutopia Newsletter,* 6–7. Retrieved August 7, 2006, from http://www.edutopia.org/EdutopiaPDF/61S98.pdf

Wenglinsky, H. (2002, February 13). How schools matter: The link between teacher classroom practices and student academic performance. *Education Policy Analysis Archives, 10(12).* Retrieved July 12, 2006, from http://epaa.asu.edu/epaa/v10n12/

Willis, S., & Mann, L. (2000). Differentiating instruction: Finding manageable ways to meet individual needs. *Curriculum Update* (Winter). Alexandria, VA: Association for Supervision and Curriculum Development. Retrieved June 8, 2006, from http://www.ascd.org/ed_topics/cu2000win_willis.html

Yackanicz, L. (2000). *Reluctant writers and writing-prompt software.* Unpublished master's thesis, Chestnut Hill College, Philadelphia, PA.

Zimmerman, W. G., & Goodman, R. H. (2001, February 1). Thinking differently about technology in our schools. *eSchool News Online.* Retrieved June 30, 2006, from http://www.eschoolnews.com/news/showStory.cfm?ArticleID=2281

Notes

Notes

Notes

Notes